DYNAMITE

WRITING

IDEAS!

EMPOWERING STUDENTS
TO BECOME AUTHORS

Melissa Forney

Maupin House

Dynamite Writing Ideas!

Book design by David Dishman
Layout design by Melissa Forney
Edited by Candace Nelson

Forney, Melissa, 1952-
Dynamite Writing Ideas! : for 2nd-6th grade teachers/ Melissa Forney--1st ed.
p.   cm.
ISBN 0-929895-18-5
1. English language--Composition and exercises--Study and teaching
(Elementary)   I.Title.
LB1576.F633   1996
372.6'23'044--dc20   96-9883
                                                        CIP

Printed in the United States of America
10 9 8 7 6 5 4 3 2

Maupin House Publishing
32 S. W. 42 Street
P.O. Box 90148
Gainesville, FL 32607
1-800-524-0634
fax: 352-373-5588
jgraddy@maupinhouse.com

DEDICATION

DEDICATED TO ALL THE TEACHERS
IN THE TRENCHES WHO ASK,

"HOW DO I GET STARTED?"

SPECIAL THANKS...

My deepest gratitude to Marcia Freeman, author, writing consultant, and friend, for her advice and undying encouragement. Her dedication to writing has reinforced my belief that teaching children to write is a noble cause.

My appreciation to Kathleen, who was my right hand while I was writing this book, to Rebecca, who cooked and guarded Big Red, and to Lucy, who kept my feet warm. I salute them all.

My greatest thanks to my husband and best friend, Rick Forney, who loved and supported me, served me Diet Dr. Pepper at the computer, and tucked me in bed, exhausted. Husband extraordinaire!

And especially to Mother, who always insisted, "You can do anything."

TABLE OF CONTENTS

Maupin House © 1996 Dynamite Writing Ideas!

KIDS AS AUTHORS

What Is Writing, Anyway?

Writing is a thought process that expresses itself in a thousand different ways. Mental creativity. Every child is a potential author, but the mystical door to self-expression has often been locked. Why? A variety of reasons. Ridicule. Lack of language arts background at home. Fear of failure. Rejection. Our job as teachers is to unlock that door.

Writing is the formulation of fresh ideas, presented in a myriad of formats. As teachers, we traditionally have presented writing as the end product, a story or report written on lined paper. However, that is *just one form* of writing. The fact that often we demanded grammatical perfection, immaculate margins, and inflexible deadlines limited the success rate. Can you imagine trying to limit painting to a paint-by-number kit? Restricting a chef to recipes that only include pasta? Asking a designer to create just from denim?

Where Does Writing Take Place?

All writing starts in a stimulating environment. In general, teachers are control freaks. To us, a stimulating environment means picture perfect bulletin boards and several "don't touch," orderly displays around the room. A "good" classroom is one where kids sit in neat rows, face the front, don't talk to their neighbors, and pay strict attention to our every word. We pride ourselves on absolute control of our subjects. Baloney!

Is your goal to have a writing community in your classroom? Then take a look at a real writing community. Just for the hands-on experience, visit your city paper's newsroom. You'll see some journalists working independently, others discussing news events with photographers or conducting interviews, a few on the phone, some using computers, and still more brainstorming in groups. These methods have proven results. That's the reality of a writing community. Why should our classrooms be different? Our job as teachers is to prepare kids for the real world.

1

What Does A Writing Classroom Look Like?

What do I hope to see when I visit a writing classroom? Contrary to what some might think, the noise level is not deafening, and there are few spitballs whizzing through the air. I see most of the students working quite independently at their desks, work tables, or computers. Two kids who are planning a drama for Black History Month enthusiastically draft a two-part dialogue between Rosa Parks and her bus driver. An ESOL student who speaks little English but is a crackerjack artist is drawing pictures for yet another boy's story. The collaborators confer occasionally while the teacher moves from group to group, validating good work procedures, giving help, noticing improvement, and managing the classroom. Creativity at its orderly best!

At such times I am overcome by the urge to celebrate. A writing classroom! The stimulation of such a creative environment makes me want to participate, write, evaluate, celebrate, respond, learn, think...

What Kind Of Teachers Do Kids Need?

Great ones! Children need exciting, creative teachers, the best available, to help them become writers and published authors. In my writing consulting business, I often run into "Super Teachers." Whether they've taught three, 12, or 32 years makes very little difference. They love children and go out of their way to help each child reach his potential as a student and writer. Most of all, they're visionaries.

Teachers who constantly are looking for improvement, innovative new techniques, and fresh ideas have the most impressive classrooms. Children hardly can wait to come to school each day to see what new experience awaits them. Best of all, these teachers are not intimidated by a stimulating learning environment. Their students thrive. The tide of knowledge ebbs and flows tantalizingly back and forth between teacher and students. Students become teachers and authors.

The ideas in this book are designed to help you become a "Super Teacher" who helps kids reach their highest potential.

What Is Motivational Teaching?

In "the old days" of **traditional teaching,** knowledge started and ended with the teacher, who had all the right answers. Students were fed facts to memorize and recall on tests or oral drills. Creativity and spontaneity were sacrificed on the altar of conformity.

Motivational teaching is designed to encourage creativity and different learning styles and enable the greatest mastery of knowledge. Notice the difference between the flow of knowledge in both methods:

TEACHER
k
n
o
w
l
e
d
g
e
STUDENTS

TRADITIONAL TEACHING

In traditional teaching, students have little input on writing topics, projects, and learning styles. Most, if not all, information, ideas, and strategies originate with the teacher. While this might be appropriate for some academic subjects, it is less than desirable for teaching a creative discipline such as writing.

MOTIVATIONAL TEACHING

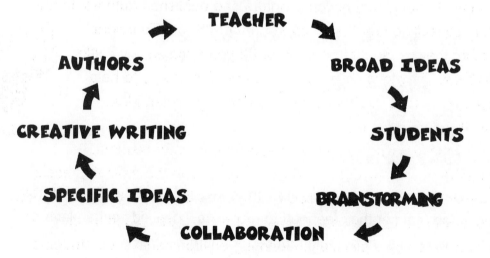

TEACHER

AUTHORS → → BROAD IDEAS

CREATIVE WRITING ← STUDENTS

SPECIFIC IDEAS ← BRAINSTORMING

COLLABORATION

In motivational teaching, kids are involved in the decision making process and become motivated to seek information from different sources, write creatively, and "publish for readers," thus becoming authors.

Is Balance Possible?

Yes, yes, yes!

The Whole Language movement introduced teachers to the concept of teaching writing through meaningful experiences. Children were encouraged to learn naturally through literature, with more emphasis placed on the creativity than the conventions. This put traditional teachers in a quandary. Aren't spelling, grammar, and conventions an integral part of writing? Won't kids need to know these skills in real-life situations? Is it possible to balance individual creativity with standard English?

The answer is yes. By using the best of both worlds, kids can become authors, feel ownership in their learning, and still learn skills such as spelling, sentence structure, and grammar.

To create balanced writers, first introduce kids to every possible genre of writing: short stories, picture books, puppet plays, poetry, speeches, classroom dramas, choral readings, wordless books, shadow boxes, chapter books, newspaper articles, phone messages, biographies, and the like.

Our job is to whet young appetites for learning, waft the aroma of stimulating writing over your students and notice the response.

Hey! This is awesome. I thought I hated poetry.

Can we do this some more? You mean, Helen Keller
      was actually a real person?

Could I read this part tomorrow?

Look what I drew!

Do we have to stop?

Next, it is important for children to investigate topics that interest them in the manner they respond to most. How can kids write plays or poetry unless they've been introduced to them before?

When it comes to a variety of literature, most children have been on a starvation diet. Fill your classroom with a plethora of writing samples and sources. These can stem from items you've collected in the past, pieces borrowed from other teachers and classrooms, library books, taped speeches, sets of classroom dramas, hanging mobiles, art projects that illustrate and enhance writing, and any other stimulating form of writing. You are presenting a menu of what kids can strive to accomplish during the coming year, a veritable smorgasbord from which to choose!

It is a particular joy to introduce kids to new authors. One key to an interest in writing is for students to "get to know" a particular author, his background, and style. Young writers are fascinated by the fact that authors are real people. If you can get kids to see themselves as authors, your battle is half won.

Kids know all published works have correct spelling, sentence structure and punctuation. Teach spelling, grammar, and conventions in the context of writing on an as-needed basis. Adjectives and transition words make a lot more sense when you're putting them to use in an actual writing piece. Let kids come up with lists of vocabulary words as they read and research new topics.

What Does A Kid Need To Become A Great Author?

- ◆ A place of his own
  - ◆ Peace and quiet
    - ◆ Uninterrupted time
      - ◆ Support from teacher/family
        - ◆ Organization
          - ◆ Writer's notebook
            - ◆ Stimulation
              - ◆ Confidence
                - ◆ Patience
                  - ◆ Creativity
                    - ◆ Secrecy
                      - ◆ Dedication & self discipline
                        - ◆ Persistence
                        - ◆ Teachable attitude
                        - ◆ Positive reinforcement
                      - ◆ To be open minded
                    - ◆ Feedback from peers
                  - ◆ Writing handouts, critique sheets
                - ◆ Personal editor/critique group
              - ◆ Record-keeping system
            - ◆ An audience
          - ◆ Assessment

NOTES:

Why Is Writing So Important?

First of all, writing is not just an extra skill tacked on to the demands of our regular academics. Along with reading, writing is the most important skill we teach throughout education. Mastering writing empowers students to express themselves and communicate for a lifetime. Teachers often ask, "How can I fit writing into my schedule? I already have so many demands put on me by the county and state, there's barely time for the other subjects I have to teach." In my opinion, that viewpoint is entirely backwards!

Written communication is the *key* to self expression and the platform for knowledge. If you teach good writing skills first, those skills will benefit kids in every content area. Teachers who tack writing on last are robbing kids of their most valuable tool.

Imagine building a beautiful home in the choicest of settings. It would be foolish to spend all your money on wallpaper and furniture but agree to settle for a cheap, weak foundation. If a home is designed properly and built of high-grade building materials, it becomes a showcase of strength, a display of beauty and can be used for many years.

A solid foundation in basic writing skills teaches kids how to assimilate knowledge on their own, evaluate, process, and express it. Children will remember only a fraction of what they learn in your classroom. However, when you empower them to express their views through writing, they continually will seek out new knowledge and have the tools for lifelong learning.

Who Are Our Kids?

In order to be an effective teacher of writing, you have to know your students. What personality characteristics do they have? Where are they in their emotional development? How are they affected by their race, culture, and family background? What writing topics interest them? What variety of learning styles do they have? Who are the leaders in the class? Who needs one-on-one attention or mentoring?

"KNOW YOUR KIDS" CHART

KINDERGARTNERS - 1ST GRADERS

Think their opinion is "it!"
Are self-centered.
Have a "Me first!" attitude
Have a short attention span
Don't like to share possessions
Believe in magic, fantasy, personification
Have a huge, active, imagination
Live in a limited "world"
Take things literally
Fear failure
Form lifelong impressions
Accept teacher as ultimate authority
Need encouragement & approval
Have a specific sense of right & wrong
Need to be read to daily
Can express themselves verbally
Have a limited written vocabulary
Have limited spelling & conventions
Like to experiment with colors
Equate literature with pictures
Need frequent modeling
Need periods of quiet
Need periods of stimulation
Like repetition and order
Will accept editing by mentor
Learn to spell while writing
Can write creatively
Love to enact and role play
Can give and receive compliments
Are hesitant to receive criticism
Need THINK time

2ND - 3RD GRADERS

Are still very firm in their own opinions
Accept that others might have
     valid differences in opinion
Live in an expanding "world"
Can distinguish between reality/fantasy
Become more organized, systematic
Accept more individual responsibility
Store knowledge/draw on knowledge
Begin to understand abstract,
     figurative meanings & stories
Need group modeling
Begin to utilize research resources
Become "story" oriented, (less "picture")
Sense of right/wrong becomes broader
Begin to look at motivation, reasoning
Fear not being "good enough"
Need encouragement, feedback
Need quiet time to read, plan, write
Respond to location, background
Still need to use their imaginations,
     move about, talk, perform
Still need to be read to
Can learn editing, error detection
Will accept editing by peers if it has been
     modeled adequately
Are motivated by "positive examples"
Accept teacher's authority over parents
Can give and receive compliments
Can give and receive criticism
Are going through emotional change
Need THINK time

4TH - 5TH GRADERS

Value the opinions of others
Are swayed by the opinions of others
Need and want to express their opinions
Broaden relationships beyond self,
     family, and school
Want to be accepted as part of the group
Can utilize research resources independently
Enjoy contemporary realistic fiction & fantasy
Want some position of authority or importance
Begin to question values, right & wrong
Can be organized, systematic, independent
Develop a long-range outlook
Accept and desire individual responsibility
Can store knowledge and teach others
Respond well to group modeling
Have highly individualized learning styles

Need quiet time to read, plan, write
Like to be read to
Can model & mentor
Still escape into fantasy
Need positive feedback from teacher
Have a fragile self image
Have a changing sense of right & wrong
Identify with characters in literature
Develop workplace/marketplace skills
Give and receive compliments
Give and receive suggestions
Question the authority of the teacher
Like teams and competition
Need lots of stimulation and motivation
Are interested in the opposite sex
Need THINK time

Grade-Appropriate Writing
KINDERGARTNERS

Speak rhymes, sing songs, chant

Repeat stories

Add details to stock story

Make up story, add details, act out story

Share an opinion, show and tell, retell an experience

Relate story to teacher for dictation

Hold writing utensil, scribble, copy pattern, copy drawing

Write mock letters, scattered letters, letter strings

Write left to right, top to bottom

Copy words from board or chart

Know and use sight words and familiar words

Construct storyboard sequence of 4 frames

Use simple transition words

Use drawings as a rehearsal for writing

Draw original artwork (static)

Begin to show movement in artwork

Define a purpose for their writing

Sit in author chair, share with class

Are able to answer questions about their writing

Become aware of self as "author"

Use writing notebook, gather information

Begin to revise stories, add on, tell more information

"Read" story to self & others

Interact with others, copy others

Write captions for drawings

Connect sounds to letters

Use inventive spelling

Begin to write short sentences

Communicate through writing & drawing

Grade-Appropriate Writing
1ST GRADERS

Keep writing notebook

Have a bank of sight words and familiar words

Still use drawing as integral part of writing process

Write complete sentences

Sequence story narrative

Use beginning transition words

Use descriptive nouns, strong verbs

Make lists

Notice details in a story

Revise work, add on

Construct storyboard sequence of 4-8 frames

Ask and answer questions concerning writing

Paraphrase stock stories in own words, add details

Think of an ending for a story, create alternative endings

Invent an original story

Select topics that are of interest to self and others

Relate interesting events

Fantasize and use imagination

Know and use simple punctuation

Hold peer conferences with fellow students

Give effective speeches, use props

Like to role play

Enjoy using puppets

Create and communicate messages

Define a purpose for their writing

Look forward to group feedback

Sit in author chair, share with class

Edit and improve their work

Communicate through writing & drawing

Grade-Appropriate Writing
2ND AND 3RD GRADERS

Use dialogue in stories
Vary sentence beginnings
Use basic punctuation
Use basic transition words
Revise writing, add on, tell more information
Like to explore a variety of art mediums
Need to be encouraged to move from drawings towards writing
Are influenced to write by the medium, style of paper, etc.
Often write their entire storyline in the title or first line
Need to talk in order to move their writing forward
Brainstorm, plan, web (with help)
Construct storyboard sequence of 8-12 frames
Use descriptive nouns, strong verbs
Write stories with beginning, middle, ending
Want to share their opinions in writing
Support opinions with facts
Write complete paragraphs (2nd) & multiple paragraphs (3rd)
Often structure sentences with "and" & lists of words
Write letters to friends and family
Write plays, poetry, diaries, & journals
Give speeches and use props
Spell commonly used words and use inventive spelling
Follow guidelines for form and neatness
Produce rough drafts and final copy
Select topics that are of interest to self and others
Use specific word choice
Combine several simple sentences into one complex sentence
Spot run-on sentences
Take many notes in order to store information
Make lists of nouns and descriptive words
Ask and answer questions concerning writing
Hold peer conferences with fellow students

Grade-Appropriate Writing
4TH AND 5TH GRADES

Write 5-paragraph essays

Use multiple characters, multidimensional characters

Write with different "voices"

Use extensive dialogue

Write with an epic viewpoint

Understand abstract themes

Write all types of letters

Write multiple-character stories (narratives)

Invent complex plots

Brainstorm, plan, web

Construct storyboard sequences of 12-16 frames

Have mastered peer and self-editing

Use all transition words

Understand and use pronoun agreement, subject/verb agreement

Proofread another writer's work as well as their own

Know basic proofreader symbols

Understand and use research resources

Write summaries & paraphrase

Develop a strong sense of having something important to say

Spot and correct run-on sentences

Use plot devices and complications

Read and write historical narratives

Read and write chapter books

Write persuasively

Compare and contrast

Are able to write and present speeches

Write dramas and portray roles

Write song lyrics

Write editorials

Express themselves through poetry

Write for publication

Take many notes in order to store information

PREPARATION

Your Classroom

Let's start at the beginning. The week before school. You've worked your fingers to the bone to prepare your room and create a perfect learning

environment. A flesh-colored blister you earned cutting and a giant cornucopia of You've arranged and and racked. Everything sanitized, scrutinized, You've scrubbed and hung, laminated and band-aid covers the out forty yellow chicks harvest vegetables. exchanged, stacked has been organized, and alphabetized. rubbed, strung and decontaminated, sliced, diced, glued and stewed until your room's a gleaming den of glory.

Norman Schwartzkoff, step aside. There's a new kid in town!

Accept the fact that your room is not going to remain this way for long. Take a Polaroid™ to remind yourself on days when kids are perched on every surface busily working with computer paper, glue, confetti, and glitter. A writing education is definitely hands-on.

Organization is the key to a productive room. Kids should feel ownership and freedom to use and explore every area of the writing classroom. However, organization and rules keep chaos from reigning.

Vital Areas of a Writing Classroom Can Include:

- Author's Chair
- Computers and Printers
- Flip Charts
- Writing Supply Center
- Art Supply Center
- Publishing Center
- Bulletin Boards

- Book and Magazine Racks
- Puppet Stage
- Filming Corner/Video Camera
- Conference Area
- Drafting Table
- Phone Line
- Reference Center

Fill Your Room With Books!

Good Sources For Classroom Literature

- garage sales
- library sales
- retiring teachers
- bookstore remainder tables
- thrift stores
- flea markets
- county school book morgues
- estate sales, other schools
- publishing companies
- charitable organizations
- little theaters

- poetry societies
- cultural exchange programs
- museums
- travel agencies
- corporate sponsors
- authors
- artists/illustrators
- software companies
- librarians
- book clubs
- private book collectors

Seating Arrangement

The arrangement of desks and chairs has a lot to do with a stimulating writing environment. Experiment. Anything goes as long as it's organized and conducive to collaboration and the maximum work space. We all find change refreshing, so be open to rearranging if the need arises. Kids love to help organize the room!

I've seen pods, teams, double circles, rows, and stations all work well. The main thing is to provide as much room as possible for kids to have work space, keep organized, and store works in progress. Writing takes place in some amazingly strange places, so don't be surprised if the bean bag chair or under the work table are hot areas. I've written some of my best pieces in the hammock under the shady carrotwood tree in my back yard.

Writing Supplies

Make your room *writer friendly*. Provide a writing-supplies area with plenty of paper, pencils, pens, felt-tip markers, highlighters, crayons, stickers, scissors, glue, tape, book binding tape, cardboard, stencils, old magazines, maps, reference materials, and work-table space. "Stuff" is cheap; *kids are valuable.*

Encourage kids to bring in items from home that can be donated to the classroom writing-supplies area. You'll double your resources and have a constant flow of interesting supplies. Children respond to different learning styles and writing mediums. Lined paper, blank books, poster paper, storyboards, comic-book squares, chalk boards, tape recorders, video cameras, stationery, and computer software are waiting to be filled with the imaginative stories of budding authors.

One teacher I know has a writing-utensils box with unusual or funny pens and pencils. This started as a hobby, and now her students donate all sorts of amazing contributions gleaned from vacations and novelty stores. She encourages her writers to check them out to see if they get any new ideas from a pencil topped with a bumblebee or a vibrating pen. I know I would!

Kids need to feel ownership in the writing-supplies area, adding supplies and organizing as needed. They should feel free to come before or after class or at a designated time to get any supplies they need. I still cringe when I hear a well-meaning teacher say, "You have no pencil, Benjy? Then you'll sit and watch while the rest of us write." She thinks she's doing Benjy a favor in the long run by depriving him of a privilege because of his lack of preparation. I would much rather include Benjy in the writing activity and provide a pencil for him. That may be the very day he would have come up with his best story yet.

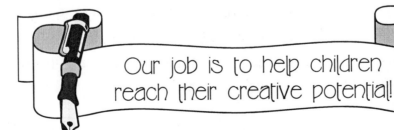

Our job is to help children reach their creative potential!

Order Writing Software

If your budget provides for writing software, familiarize yourself with the program before you order by visiting a class or school where it's actually being used. You also can enlist the help of your school media specialist or writing-lab consultant. Your teacher workroom should have catalogues galore to choose from, but remember, *try out software before ordering.*

Writing software has a dazzling effect on any writer. Even the most reluctant kid can't resist the special effects and ready-to-use illustrations. Lots of programs give kids the ability to interact with characters on the screen, come up with their own plots, add sound, and then present their stories to the rest of the class in video format.

Most educational software is affordable and can be ordered and installed in a matter of days if you have the means to pay up front. A great way to immerse yourself in the software world is to attend an educational-software multimedia convention in your area.

Enlist Volunteers

I am always appalled at the desperate need most schools have for classroom volunteers. Unless your school is very unusual, it always could use more willing helpers who have the kids' best interest at heart. Principal Kris Bayer has enlisted the help of 99 active volunteers who visit his school several times each week. What a windfall for his 600 kids!

Volunteers are like any other work force—they must be trained. If your school policy permits, round up several willing adults to help with student writing, give them specific jobs and detailed instruction, and you'll wonder how you ever taught without them. Don't overlook senior citizens.

I schedule a few night sessions with my volunteers and over light refreshments, train them how to help publish, encourage, proofread, and a few other writing basics. I stress how important volunteers are and how much the children and I count on their regular help. They fill out their own schedules and that way I know exactly when to expect them.

What is the key to successful volunteers? Have plenty for them to do and make sure their efforts are rewarded with praise and appreciation.

"HELP!!!"

Letter To Kids

A great way to prepare your students for a positive writing experience is to send a letter to them during the summer and invite them to write back. Teachers who take the time to do this agree that it really pays off. If you have the use of a computer, it's easy to write a group letter and add a personal note at the bottom. Use the following example or create your own. Send early enough to allow kids to respond.

DEAR JULIE,
I HOPE YOUR SUMMER IS GOING WELL. I CAN'T WAIT TO SEE YOU THIS FALL AT SCHOOL.

DEAR JASON,

I'M THE LUCKY PERSON WHO GETS TO BE YOUR 3RD GRADE TEACHER THIS COMING YEAR AT NORTH SHORE ELEMENTARY. OUR ROOM IS #310, RIGHT ACROSS FROM THE LIBRARY.

WE'LL BE DOING LOTS OF WRITING IN OUR CLASS THIS YEAR, SO I'D LIKE YOU TO THINK OF A FEW SUBJECTS THAT INTEREST YOU. HOBBIES, ANIMALS, FUNNY STUFF, SPORTS, NATURE, CURRENT EVENTS ARE JUST A FEW THINGS KIDS LIKE. I WANT TO MAKE SURE WE HAVE LOTS TO WRITE ABOUT, SO PLEASE SEND ME A LIST AND I'LL LOOK FOR PICTURES AND MAGAZINES.

WHEN YOU SEND THE LIST, WOULD YOU TELL ME A LITTLE ABOUT YOURSELF? I LIKE TO KNOW THE KIDS IN MY ROOM. YOU CAN DRAW A PICTURE OR SEND A PHOTO IF YOU LIKE. I LOVE GETTING MAIL.

I LIVE NEAR THE BEACH AND I SOMETIMES RIDE JET SKIS. MY FAVORITE FOOTBALL TEAM IS THE FLORIDA GATORS. I LIKE SCARY MOVIES, ICE COLD COKES, AND POPCORN. NOW YOU KNOW SOME THINGS ABOUT ME.

IF YOU'RE ALREADY WRITING THIS SUMMER, FEEL FREE TO BRING ANY STORIES OR POEMS WITH YOU. WE'VE GOT A BIG BULLETIN BOARD AND I WANT TO FILL IT WITH STUFF KIDS WRITE.

SEE YOU IN AUGUST!

Letter To Parents

The most successful teaching experience I've ever had actually was with parents. I invited them to come to school one night and take a two-hour class in writing so they could help their kids at home. I didn't know what the turnout would be, but there was standing room only.

Before school begins, prepare a letter to send to parents after the first few days of school. Keep them constantly informed about the writing progress in your classroom, and you'll gain their support and enthusiasm.

Dear Parents,

Our classroom is going to incorporate writing into almost every subject we learn and the projects we do this year. It's a great way to prepare your child for a college education and a successful career. I'll keep you informed as to how you can be a real encouragement at home. Writers have special needs, but they're special people.

You won't be seeing as many papers come home on Fridays. Don't worry! It takes longer to work on editing and improvement when you're teaching kids to do their very best. We're using a Writer's Notebook system this year so we can pull spelling and vocabulary words from the subjects we're studying and the books we're reading. I'll schedule a time with each of you to come in to see your child's progress. You're welcomed to attend our Writing Workshops any morning. It's the most important time of day.

Bulletin Boards and Displays

Every writing classroom needs several prominent places where kids' work can be displayed. Lower, accessible bulletin boards help encourage kids to read what others have written. Don't be afraid to put up work in all different stages. This can be a valuable tool to dispel the old "work has to be perfect to be displayed" myth. Involve your class in designing, filling, and changing bulletin boards with student work.

Encourage students to contribute jokes, riddles, poems, captions, interesting facts, stories, news events, etc. Locate bulletin boards near doorways so kids can read while waiting in line. Hang a small bulletin board over a classroom water fountain or by the pencil sharpener. If your school encourages hallway bulletin boards, showcase student writing.

NOTES:

Last Minute Reminders

✓ **Order classroom newspaper** - Many city newspapers supply free newspapers or provide a low educational rate for classroom students. Lessons on current events, weather, trends, ads, interviews, etc., are valuable tools for young writers.

✓ **Plan field trips** - Schools often require advance notice and planning for off-campus trips. Consider which units lend themselves to field trips and plan writing projects to coincide.

✓ **Request equipment** - Be sure to let your media specialist know when you'll need overhead, opaque projector, video camera, film, 35mm cameras, television, VCR, tape recorder, microphone, sound system, etc. If these are available, ask to reserve them for pre-arranged dates and make sure they're in working order. Sometimes school districts have far more equipment than any one school and are willing to lend.

✓ **Book a tour of the school media center** - Media specialists are often the most overworked employees and seldom have a chance to get to know individual kids. Make a reservation for a guided tour as soon as it can be scheduled. Bring flowers and make a special effort to point out how helpful the media specialist can be for writers.

✓ **Line up guest speakers** - Your community is probably teeming with experts and interesting individuals who'd love to visit your classroom as a guest speaker. These visits are also a wealth of opportunities for kids to interview, take notes, ask questions, and write follow-up thank-you letters. Local newsletters, letters to the editor, church bulletins, libraries, civic clubs, and community leaders can help supply lists of possibilities.

✓ **Locate pen pals** - Writing to school children in Australia, Italy, or even to another class in your city gets children fired up about writing. Plan these activities ahead of time and coordinate with reciprocating teachers how these projects will be carried out.

✓ **Enlist local sponsors** - If you have the blessing of your school principal, just before school is a good time to enlist corporate sponsors for special writing projects. For instance, one teacher I know received 35mm disposable "weekend" cameras and developing for each of her students to use in a photo journalism essay.

ORGANIZATION 3

The Self-Contained Writer's Notebook

Over the years, I've experimented with gazillions of ways to keep student writing organized. Journals fell apart, folders wilted, and spiral notebooks became dog-eared, dangerous weapons. My students and I tried writing in different folders or notebooks for each subject. This was often confusing when trying to teach revisions, comparisons, and editing.

Was there a way to keep all student writing organized, for once and for all, I wondered? My students needed something sturdy, portable, non-expendable, with limitless pages. I finally came up with the idea of a three ring notebook to be used for *all writing*, even across the disciplines. The Self-Contained Writer's Notebook was born.

My young writers are inspired by having an author's notebook with multiple sections and crucial materials within reach. This strategy has saved countless hours of frustration and now has been implemented successfully in hundreds of classrooms. Here's what you'll need:

SUPPLIES

- clear plastic covered, colored, three-ring notebook
- #2 pencils, cap eraser, 21" piece of twine (not mono-filament)
- greenbar computer paper, cut to size, and hole punched
- lined notebook paper
- eight dividers with colored tabs
- small pad of self-stick notes (2" x 1.5")
- three-ring dictionary and thesaurus
- yellow fluorescent marker
- cover sheet, About the Author sheet, spine strip, divider strips

Approximate cost per student: $5.00

Investment: Notebooks can be used for several years, following students from grade to grade or recycled for new students.

Advantages: Notebooks can be taken on field trips, to assemblies, outside for field work, etc. Handouts and extra pages can be added easily.

The Clear Plastic Marquee

The clear plastic cover on your self-contained writer's notebooks not only will help keep them clean, but will provide a wonderful display marquee. In the front of the notebook, display a professional looking, customized front cover. This sends the message to students that this notebook is as important as any textbook, not to be doodled on or kicked around. Easily designed on the computer, the front cover can be as fancy as your imagination allows. Or better yet, let a talented student or parent create the design. At any rate, they need to display the author's name, teacher's name, and school name.

The back cover can be used as a prominent display area, changed many times during the year. I usually start with an About The Author sheet and rotate new-unit vocabulary words, seasonal pieces, or writing tips. Kids are great at coming up with new ideas for the back covers.

Notebook Assembly

The day kids receive their writer's notebooks is memorable. In advance, I enlist the help of parents and volunteers to prepare and put notebooks together assembly style.

1. Slip in front and back covers
2. Slip in spine strip
3. Tie twine to pencil and tie to bottom ring of notebook
4. Insert divider strips and add eight dividers to notebook
5. Cut greenbar paper to size, remove computer printer strips, punch holes, and add to manuscript section
6. Add supply of lined notebook paper to Idea Bank, Word Bank, Name Bank, First Line Banks and Reference Section
7. Slip fluorescent marker in notebook pocket.
8. Add dictionary, thesaurus, spelling words, vocabulary words, writing handout sheets, etc.

I wait to present writer's notebooks until I meet with students in small groups. After ingraining the importance of organization, I make a big deal out of "Notebook Day" with all the fanfare I can muster, as this marks a new beginning for our writing community.

Spine Strips

Duplicate and cut spine strips from heavier gauge paper. Print the name of each writer on a spine strip using black felt-tip marker. Bend back the flaps of the notebook before trying to insert spine strips. They will slip in easily. Now each writer has his very own personalized notebook.

Divider Strips

Duplicate divider strips from heavier gauge paper for each writer. Kids can cut out their own divider strips and slip them in the divider tabs.

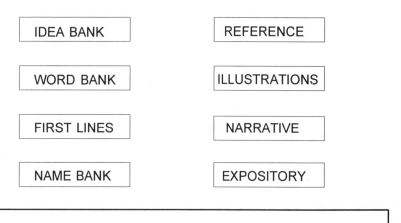

IDEA BANK	REFERENCE
WORD BANK	ILLUSTRATIONS
FIRST LINES	NARRATIVE
NAME BANK	EXPOSITORY

Writer's Name _____

✂ cut here --

Spine Strips

Duplicate and cut spine strips from heavier gauge paper. Print the name of each writer on a spine strip using black felt-tip marker. Bend back the flaps of the notebook before trying to insert spine strips. They will slip in easily. Now each writer has his very own personalized notebook.

Divider Strips

Duplicate divider strips from heavier gauge paper for each writer. Kids can cut out their own divider strips and slip them in the divider tabs.

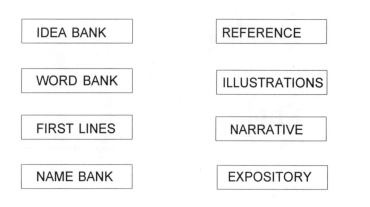

IDEA BANK	REFERENCE
WORD BANK	ILLUSTRATIONS
FIRST LINES	NARRATIVE
NAME BANK	EXPOSITORY

Writer's Name _____

Your School Name

Writer's Notebook

Author's Name

_____

Teacher

_____

Grade

_____

Room

_____

About the Author

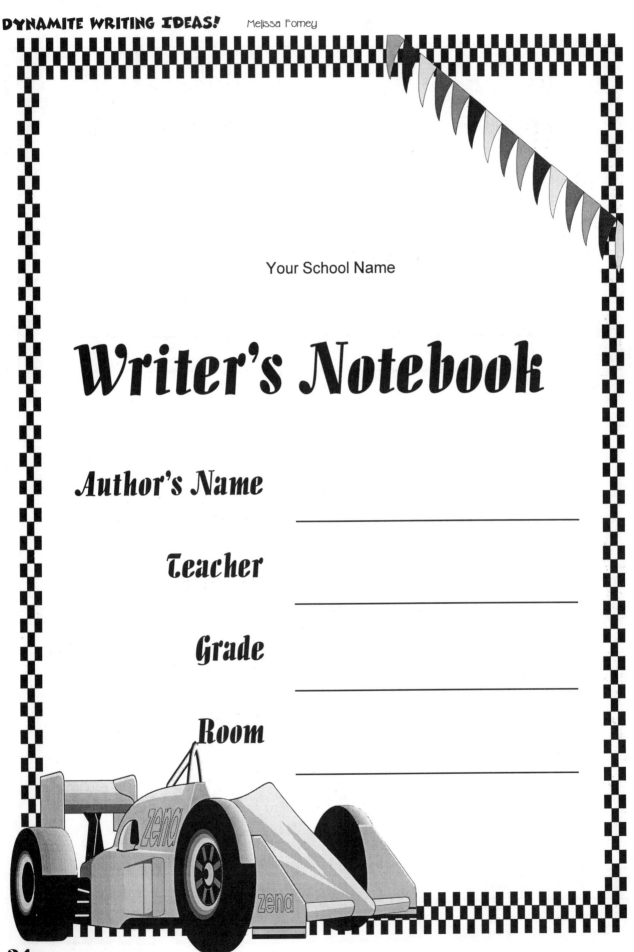

Your School Name

Writer's Notebook

Author's Name

_____

Teacher

_____

Grade

_____

Room

_____

About the Author

_____

_____

_____

_____

_____

_____

_____

_____

_____

_____

_____

_____

Idea Bank

Writing teachers share a common nightmare. While others dream of winning the lottery or being stuck on a South Sea island with Mel Gibson, our dream is terrifying. We are standing in the middle of the classroom trying to inspire our charges to new heights of writing skill. Suddenly we are surrounded by a multitude of doubters, each whining, "I don't know what to write about." We wake in a cold sweat. Where is Mel when we need him?

Kids are more than capable of coming up with great topics to write about. The problem, however, is we have no forewarning when ideas are going to strike. The number one question I'm asked as an author is where I get my ideas. Ideas can come at any time—on our way home from school, while washing dishes, or even when someone else is speaking.

The key for writers is to capture the ideas when they first appear. Instead of hushing the kid who's waving his hand furiously when another child has the floor, teach him to jot down his idea or point of view on a sticky-note. Once this becomes a habit, students develop the insight of capturing their ideas for later use.

My students and I compile huge lists of ideas, often brainstorming as we go. Since ideas spark other ideas, we get out our writing notebooks and turn to the Idea Bank section before discussions. We usually do this in the late afternoon when we are tired from other activities. I'll simply ask, "What are some things that interest you, or new stuff you've learned? Let's talk." Before the bell rings we have lots of new ideas.

When Missy mentions the fact that her grandmother is teaching her to quilt, Tiffany is reminded that she is learning to crochet. She then writes down the word crochet in her idea book and mentions, "My mother is teaching me to crochet." Talking about grandmothers reminds Ryan that he will be taking care of a pony at his grandmother's farm the coming summer, a fact he is very excited about. "I'm going to learn how to take care of a horse," he announces, jotting it down in his Idea Bank at the same time.

And so it goes, the collecting of idea after idea. All topics kids are interested in are stored as possible writing topics for future workshops.

Some kids accrue dozens of subjects, far more than they ever actually will write about. That's great. They're thinking like writers. When someone really doesn't have any idea what to write about, the class always can brainstorm on the spot to help him out. This builds camaraderie and fosters critical thinking.

Ideas come from magazine articles, movies, videos, discussions, arguments, family activities, growing pains, accomplishments, losses, triumphs, or topics of keen interest. We find out lots about each other by sharing ideas. When Kevin mentions that he is interested in shark fishing, six or seven other kids might say, "Cool! I am, too!" adding that topic to their Idea Banks as well. I hear other comments such as "Could I borrow that idea?" and "You made me think of something else I can write about." Kids look forward to writing time when they are armed with a whole bank of interesting ideas.

If a student's notebook is handy, he can write his idea right in the Idea Bank. When the class is doing another activity or listening to a speaker, he can use a sticky-note pad to "capture" the idea until his writer's notebook is handy. *Voila! Not a single idea lost!*

Word Bank

Scrumptious Idea... Decidedly Delectable!

I *love* words. I've been having a "word affair" all my life. I like to look at them, sound them out, know their meanings and origins. Words are to be savored, repeated, collected. If I can pass the passion for selecting just the right word on to my students, they're hooked for life.

Kids like to collect things, right? Why not words? This section of the Self-Contained Writer's Notebook is for just that purpose. Instead of discarding old spelling tests and vocabulary lists, store them in the Word Bank. When you introduce content words for a new theme or unit of study, encourage your students to keep copies of these words in their Word Bank for instant reference. It might surprise you how many times they'll use these very words in their writing if they have them at their fingertips. Brainstorm lists of synonyms; neat sounding words; long, juicy words. They'll show up in student writing, thus increasing your kids' vocabularies.

First Line Bank

All writers have writer's block occasionally. Kids usually get stuck on the first line and waste long periods of time trying to think of a perfect opening sentence. In the meantime, their creativity level is steadily dropping, and their frustration level is nearing meltdown. The First Line Bank is an innovative idea that solves that problems nicely.

It works like this: I arrange to take my class to the media center and ask them to bring their Self-Contained Writer's Notebooks. In advance, I give them each a ticket, announcing there will be a prize for every kid who has a ticket at the end of the session. We make a game out of the fact that not one word can be spoken. Talkers lose their tickets.

While in the media center, kids spread out all over the place, notebooks in hand and pencils to the ready. At the signal, each begins to pull out a single book at a time, copy down the first line, and replace the book in exactly the same spot it was found. My students visit sections of the stacks they would never have noticed. The object is to collect as many first sentences as time allows. They are extraordinarily quiet and I look good in front of the media specialist and rival teachers.

The grand prize winners are the students who have collected the most first lines, the funniest, the longest, most original, scariest, etc. Every student who still has a ticket also receives a small prize. Before the end of the day or later in the week, I give kids a chance to copy first lines from each other and encourage them to add new ones.

Now students have a collection of first lines written by professional authors.  I am not encouraging plagiarism, but imitation. This is the same technique as taking art students to a museum to learn from the masters. The next time my budding writers get stuck on first sentences, I send them to their First Line Banks to see if they get any ideas. They come up with brilliant ways to change a few words around or adapt a line to their topics, and away they go. Pretty soon they are more than able to come up with their own first sentences. We also use their collections of first lines to look for descriptive words and sentence beginning variations.

Name Bank

Young writers often get bogged down in their writing efforts when it comes to naming characters. They have a limited pool from which to draw: family members, characters on their mothers' soap operas, heroes in movies or books, action figures, friends, and classmates. A collection of multi-cultural and multi-ethnic names is a valuable tool for any writer. Collect names as a class. Share new finds and update lists often. What a great opportunity for kids to research ancestral history, family trees, and cultural diversity.

In my classroom, we keep a running list of names. We like some just because of the way they sound: *Lugie Brown, Billy Burpwater, Plemon Ming, Delmer Stanfield, Chiefa Hathcock, Stuz Plunk, Dessa Rose, Nadja Van Hoose, Wylene Wilkins.* Others come from bygone eras: *Betty, Art, Thelma, Hannah, Thaddeus, Theodore, Bing, Elenore, Edgar, Alice, Melvin.* Ethnic names are particularly fun to collect: *Angus, Ian, Hansi, Mei-Ling, Lars, Collum, Kulumbu, Hang, T-Pat, Francesca, Ludwig, Massimo, Angelica, Elmer, Pepe, Kosiko, Casimir, Magda, Niles, Gunter.*

Young writers become avid collectors of names while becoming aware of the benefit of selecting just the right names for their characters. The list is readily available in their Self-Contained Writer's Notebooks when writing inspiration strikes.

Reference Section

Family members are more likely to write thank-you notes when stationery, address book, pen, and stamps are within reach.

This same theory holds true with young writers and reference materials. A student who dreads looking up words in the classroom dictionary will readily use a notebook dictionary or thesaurus that is three-hole punched and in the reference section of her notebook. You can purchase inexpensive editions through classroom book-order clubs.

As you study other disciplines and subjects, make available important information such as lists of past presidents, charts, authors, measurements, state names, capitols, maps, quotes, and holidays.

Illustrations

Call it human nature, call it habit, but the truth is, most books *are* judged by their covers. Art sells. Try this experiment: take your kids to the children's book section of any local library and ask them to select ten books that instantly appeal to them. Chances are, cover illustrations and color selections powerfully influence their choices.

On the elementary school level we do a great job of exposing children to art education and appreciation, but I seldom see illustration taught on a practical application level. ***In developing writers, there is a direct correlation between learning to draw and developing an overpowering enthusiasm for writing.***

Do you want to get kids excited about writing? One way is to teach them to draw! Most of the drawing they've done has been picked up by osmosis or by copying another kid's idea or technique. In my workshops, I sandwich a few drawing lessons between say, a lesson on descriptive writing or how to write a scary adventure story. They draw. They write.

Bada-Bing-Bada-Boom—they're hooked!

In his book, ***Imagination Station***, artist and teacher Mark Kistler writes, "I can't think of anything more beneficial to your child's self-esteem and intellectual development than a strong foundation in elementary art. Schools that harness the power of art into their core curriculum turn out children that are much happier, more confident, and better equipped intellectually to face the rigors of higher schooling."

Drawing Helps Young Writers:

...Tell A Story
...Express Emotion
...Expand Imagination
...Increase Self Esteem
...Become Self-Motivated
...Stimulate Critical Thinking
...Learn To Follow Directions
...Improve Hand-Eye Coordination
...Develop An Appreciation For Art
...Communicate Without Inhibitions
...Learn To Think Three-Dimensionally

ON YOUR MARK...

The First Month Of School

The love of writing is caught more than taught. Children will take their cue from you. If writing is presented as a wonderful form of self expression and a fascinating source of information, kids will pick it up quicker than you can say, "Take out your pencils and paper."

First impressions are powerful. When children enter your room at the beginning of the year they should sense right away that writing plays a major part in everything they do. Your first job is to convince kids writing is wonderful and has a valid purpose.

How do I get started? This is the number one question I am asked. Show kids what's available. Schedule a morning writing time the first four weeks of school and make writing activities a priority. I recommend introducing students to a sampler of every kind of written communication.

Read aloud. Pass out scripts and let your students perform fun classroom dramas. Review speeches, scenes from videos, newsreels, newspapers, letters to the editor, etc. Your goal is hands-on experience. Kids should sample as many forms of written ideas as possible. Notice how students respond differently to each genre.

During the rest of the year, when you suggest writing a radio script, your students will remember the morning they sat in a circle laughing, trying out various parts from a radio soap opera. Kids will be familiar with limericks because they'll remember the silly ones that cracked up the whole class that first week of school. The words *drama, choral reading,* and *editorial* will conjure up warm memories of shared experiences.

The first four weeks of school are the perfect opportunity for young writers to engage in critical thinking and value judgements. Not all genres of writing will appeal to everyone. Terrific! Vivé la différence!

WRITER'S SURVEY

Use the following survey to stimulate discussion, conversation and writing. It's a good way to break the ice and foster bonding. Kids can put it in their Self-Contained Writer's Notebook for future reference.

WRITER'S SURVEY

The most important thing in my bedroom is …

The best movie I ever saw was …

What scares me most is …

If I could spend one day with any person on Earth, it would be …

The last book I read was …

My favorite author is …

The neatest pet to own would be …

Two books I remember reading when I was little are …

My favorite bedtime story of all times is …

If I could live in a foreign country for three months, I'd choose …

The sport I'd like to be great at is …

My mom always tells me I'm …

The most boring thing in the world to me is …

I had a dream once that …

If I owned my own video camera, I'd really like to film …

I think the president should …

One thing that really irritates me is …

The last time I got in trouble was because …

One thing I'd really like to learn in school this year is …

My family has fun when we …

I'll never forget the time …

The most important thing I've ever done is …

One thing I'll never do is …

I like to work in a group with someone who is …

My dad taught me how to …

If I won $1,000, I'd spend it on …

When I grow up, I'd like to be …

If I could write a letter to anyone in the world, I'd write …

I'd like to be famous because of my …

If I could study anything, I'd learn how to …

Grouping Your Students

During the first four weeks of school, observe your students carefully and experiment with different groupings. Kids have individual needs and often require one-on-one attention. This attention does not always have to come from the teacher. Peers, student "experts," multi-age leaders, group members, mentors, and partners can all meet specific needs.

As a rule of thumb, I use the following system for grouping:

By skill levels - when teacher functions as facilitator within the group or when specific skills are being introduced or remediated

Heterogeneously - when teacher models before all groups or when the entire class is involved in the learning process

In Pairs - when students are working collaboratively and teacher circulates among the large group

Become A "Fellow Author" With Your Students

The most successful classroom writing environments I've seen are those where the teachers involve themselves in writing and become authors along with their students. Kids especially love to read, critique, and edit something their teacher has written. Your involvement as a fellow author will make children feel comfortable and give you first-hand experience with what you are asking your students to do on a daily basis.

As much as possible, participate as a colleague in classroom writing activities. Share your successes and failures. Dispel the myth that "teachers are always perfect" by allowing kids to see your imperfections. This camaraderie pays off as students sense an atmosphere of safety and respect and are encouraged to take new risks without the fear of failure.

Teaching writing skills in small groups is a recipe for success!

Using The Partner Clock

Here's a great idea that will help save time and stress throughout the entire year. Give each student a copy of the Partner Clock. Ask kids to make an "appointment" with someone else at each of the times listed. Both students sign each other's clock at the correct appointment time.

Every student will have four different "appointments," each with a different student. Anytime you'd like to group students quickly in partners, you can announce, "Please get with your 6:00 appointment," and so on. I encourage kids to consider who will be the best partner to work with, as we keep partners for an entire semester before changing. If a student is absent, I fill in as his partner or match him with another "spare."

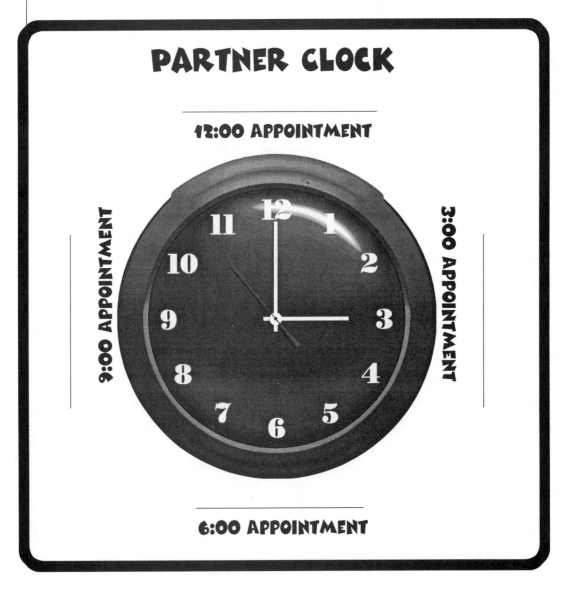

PARTNER CLOCK

12:00 APPOINTMENT

9:00 APPOINTMENT

3:00 APPOINTMENT

6:00 APPOINTMENT

First-Month Writing Activities

Before you get into the technical aspects of writing and becoming an author, it's good to discover the sheer fun of writing individually, in pairs, and in groups.

Newspaper Scavenger Hunt - Write several different categories of newspaper articles on the board. As kids read through the city newspaper, let them list articles under the proper heading or find specific information listed on the board. Sports, obituaries, editorials, world news, etc.

Write to a Famous Person - Bring in a celebrity address book and let kids sign up to write letters, one letter per celebrity. Stick map pins on a class map to show where letters have been sent and post celebrity letters that arrive on a bulletin board for all to enjoy.

Puppet Plays - Divide students into small groups and ask each group to choose a nursery rhyme, fairy tale, or another familiar story. Kids make puppets to go along with their story, practice, and present to the class.

Writing Posters - Divide students into small groups and provide poster paper, magazines, and markers. Ask each group to cut out pictures that show ways writing is necessary in our society. Write captions and present the posters to the class for discussion.

Listen to Books on Tape - Most public libraries and many school media centers offer a wide selection of children's books on tape. Interactive book software for use with classroom computers is a nice companion activity that provides an opportunity for kids to work together.

A Day in the Life Of - Kids write down all activities they do on a specific date, illustrate the account with drawings or photos, and display.

Hanging Rhyme List - This is a good activity for kids to work in groups. Make giant posters of rhyming words and hang from ceiling or on classroom walls. These come in handy for writing poetry and song lyrics.

Concrete Body Prose - Working in pairs, kids lightly trace in pencil each other's bodies on long sheets of butcher paper. Each person then writes significant words that describe his physical description and personality all around the edges of the tracing. Kids can color, cut out, or glue on poster paper and display behind their chairs or on a bulletin board. This makes a nice presentation for Parents' Night.

Magnifying-Glass Description - Take a class trip to the fresh outdoors, equipping each child with a magnifying glass and notebook. Kids pick objects, inspect them closely through the magnifying-glass, and take notes. Later, compare descriptions with class members and discuss. This is a great lesson to point out how writer's use different styles and also how important descriptive words are.

Movie Review - Let kids volunteer to review different movies at home or movies they plan to see during the weekend. Illustrate by drawing an exciting scene from the movie or present a review orally to the class. Encourage kids to come up with a class-wide rating system for plots and to make value judgements.

Helium-Balloon Message - This is fun if there are no restrictions in your area. Kids write a message asking the finder to contact your school to record exactly how far the balloon traveled. Pinpoint on a map.

Party Invitation - Let kids work in teams or groups to design a fictional party. They come up with a theme, games, refreshments, times, etc., and design party invitations that include all important information. Present to the class for discussion and comparisons.

Plan a Trip - Once again kids work in small groups to plan a fictional trip for the entire class. Using maps, brochures, travel materials, etc., they plan the destination, route, transportation, costs, entertainment, sight-seeing, etc., and write a travel brochure telling all about it. Present these to the class for discussion and post them on the bulletin board.

Weather Report/Current Events - Let kids take turns being "weather man" by writing and presenting a brief summary of the weather and/or current events. This can be presented informally, or you can ask a talented parent or student to design a "television" that kids can get inside and role play. This activity also lends itself well to interview techniques and also to train kids how to use the video camera.

Product Commercial - This activity gets really silly but is always a class favorite. Ask kids to bring unusual or made up "products" from home (air-conditioned pajamas, bubble bath for dogs, edible toothbrush, candy for goldfish, etc.) and to write commercials for them detailing their use, need, price, availability, etc. The use of costumes, music, and props provide fun and foster collaborative brainstorming and presentation.

10 WRITING MINI-LESSONS FOR LITTLE FOLKS

1. Tap and Tell

Begin telling a story in a small group. At a certain point, tap the next person, and it's her turn to continue the story. Each kid says one or two sentences before tapping the next child.

2. Shout the Noun

Before telling a story, gather props mentioned in the plot in a pillowcase. As you tell the story, pull out each prop instead of saying the noun. Kids listen and shout out the noun as you pull out the prop.

3. Story Sequence

Divide a story into 12-20 sentences. Type or write each sentence on strips of paper. Number strips and give each strip to a child. This works well if kids are able to read simple sentences. If not, there's nothing wrong with a little rehearsal! Have kids sit in order and read the story aloud to the rest of the class. If time permits, kids then may tap someone else to read in their places and the class rereads the story.

4. Story Vest

Children draw the action of a story on a paper vest. They wear the vest while telling the story to the class, leaving their hands free to point to the pictures.

5. What Do I See?

Students go on a "field trip" in the classroom, the hallway, around the school, or outside. They experience looking at many objects through a magnifying glass, pair of binoculars, tube of paper, specially-colored sunglasses, a long cardboard tube, telescope, etc. Their task is to describe what they see through the changed viewpoint.

6. Action Illustrations

Teacher shows a number of illustrations that show action vs. static drawing. Then teach kids how to draw action when illustrating their own stories. A shining sun with rays, drops of rain, arrows, "movement circles," forward "wooshes," a crying face, a laughing face, figures stepping instead of just standing. Believe it or not, teaching motion illustration actually encourages kids to add action (verbs) to their stories. If they can draw to express their feelings, they'll write to add details.

7. Whose Shoes?

Gather one of many types of shoes: baby shoe, ballet slipper, ancient tennis shoe, work boot, bedroom slipper, glittery high heel, golf shoe, cowboy boot, etc. Discuss and describe the person who would wear each shoe. The rule: you have to use a complete sentence in answering! After you've modeled this, allow more kids to have turns by dividing them up into pairs.

8. Candy Comparison

Assemble as many different kinds of candy bars as money permits. No fair eating before the lesson! Keep these in a box to build the mystery. One by one, each kid may select a bar and tell why it's his favorite, or may compare one bar with another. Bars also may be used to teach specific description words.

9. Wordless Books

Student selects a wordless book and studies it for a while to decipher the storyline. Student then may tell the story to the class, showing the illustrations, or may write the story.

10. Paragraph Writing

Teach kids the simple concept that a paragraph is made up of sentences about the same subject. Hold up a football and ask the class to write aloud. Model several other props. Then ask students to work in pairs.

GET SET...

TEACHING IN SMALL GROUPS

The Next Six Weeks

As discussed in Chapter Four, writing is a technical skill, best learned with one-on-one help. The small group is less intimidating, and kids get much more individual attention from the teacher. They ask more questions and stay on task better. New concepts and writing techniques are easier to grasp. I make sure I am seated within easy reach of each kid, so I can see work, field questions, give help, and keep my writers on task.

After the first four weeks of exposure to a variety of language arts experiences, it is time for action! Divide your class into small groups of five to eight students. Starting with a group of brighter students first can be a help in modeling, setting the tone, and boosting your success rate.

Assign the rest of your students an activity to work on at their seats and help them get started. Then ask a select group to sit at the writing conference table. Sit in the middle so you can reach each child. You already will have prepared some **props** that are on the table for discussion. I recommend keeping these props in labeled boxes for future use or sharing with other teachers. You can never have too many.

Examples of props:

Hats: sailor, nurse, bonnet, cowboy, farmer, firefighter, police officer, fedora, straw, silly, clown, ringmaster, etc.

Shoes: ballet slipper, basketball, golf, booties, sandal, dressy, bedroom slipper, clogs, dirty old sneaker, high heel, etc.

Medical: hypodermic syringe, thermometer, bandages, ice pack, tongue depressor, stethoscope, alcohol, splints, etc.

Bottles: baby, water, canteen, shampoo, ketchup, ink, perfume, soda, vanilla flavoring, milk, vitamin drops, glue, etc.

Joining together with other teachers to collect an assortment of prop boxes is a good idea and means less work for everybody. Use your imagination to come up with interesting and unusual objects. Parents and volunteers can help select items kids would really be interested in seeing.

In the small group, encourage students to identify, touch, examine, and investigate props and to answer questions. Stimulate pre-writing discussion and validate creative, critical thinking.

Prop Discussion Questions:

Who would use this? Why? What is it called?

Which of these would you carry in the trunk of your car? Why?

Describe the person who would wear this. Where did she get it?

If you had to buy this, where would you find it? What would it cost?

Compare this…to this…What are the similarities? Differences?

Which of these is the scariest? Funniest? Most useful? Why?

If you were stuck by yourself on an island, which of these would you want to have with you? Why?

Other students in the room will overhear these discussions while you are working with the small group. This is beneficial. I usually try to place kids who need extra help, or haven't had many successes, in the last small group. By their turn they've heard the discussion several times before and can share answers. We are "programming" their success.

Ask students to pick a prop to write about at home or during writing time when you will work with another small group. Model the kind of writing you'd like to see and show samples of student writing. Let kids have copies, if possible, or read examples. Discuss which ones are well written and why. Use highlighters to call attention to new skills.

Repeat these steps with each small group. You may use the same props or a variety of different ones but keep the discussions and writing skills along the same lines. Your goal is to teach the same knowledge to the entire class while being able to give individual attention to each child. Before you start each day, be sure to get the other students on track with writing activities so they'll be working while you teach the small group. I use props at the beginning of the year and occasionally bring them out again during writing workshops to rekindle enthusiasm and interest.

SKILLS TO TEACH IN SMALL GROUP

SOCIAL GRACES

- giving and receiving compliments
- giving and receiving constructive criticism
- giving and receiving suggestions
- listening while others are speaking
- following and giving directions
- working with a partner
- teaching a new skill to another student
- collaborating as a group or team
- being a gracious loser in a game
- using a soft voice when in pairs
- respecting the opinions of others
- not making fun of others or their ideas
- reading your writing piece aloud

WRITING TECHNIQUE

- prewriting
- rough draft
- descriptive writing
- strong verbs
- introductions
- conclusions
- inventing a problem
- character development
- balancing a solution
- sequential plot
- staying focused
- supportive details
- transition words
- peer conferencing
- revising
- editing

WRITING MECHANICS

- vary sentence beginnings
- indent paragraphs
- beginning punctuation
- end punctuation
- proofreading
- proper nouns
- quotation marks
- commas
- skipping lines
- spelling
- margins

GENRES

- short stories
- autobiography
- opinion
- persuasion
- how to
- factual report
- journalism
- poetry
- fiction

CONCEPTS

- inventive spelling
- 1st view
- 3rd view
- mood
- tone
- flashbacks
- foreshadowing
- complications
- fantasy
- realism
- setbacks

Training Student Editors

I don't know of a teacher, anywhere, who has enough time to get everything done. Because we're constantly trying to keep our heads above water, it's difficult to find time to edit student writing. Training a few kids to become student editors is one way to free you up to handle the more critical writing where a teacher's expertise is necessary.

Select several students who are "quick studies" and work well with other kids. Schedule a time to train them as a small group, possibly during lunch or before school. The three or four sessions you'll devote to them will pay off all year long, as they assist you and their classmates.

I use duplicated examples of student writing from previous years and equip my would-be editors with colored pens and highlighters. We check over the papers, looking for obvious errors or omissions. I model how to circle errors with pen and highlight omissions so we're all using the same methods of correction. In a short while they become good at it. Another part of my training is the instilling of professionalism, honesty, and the desire to help others, all qualities that will pay off in real life.

I pin my "graduates" in a short ceremony in front of the class. They wear the badges during writing workshops when they are available to edit student work. Editors are still responsible for their own writing so they come in before school or take things home to finish. Before students have an appointment with me to asses their writing, they first must "pass" and be stamped by a Student Editor. This step saves me from wasting teacher time on petty things such as no name or end punctuation!

When I get the student editors running smoothly, I choose a few more kids to train. This time when we meet, however, I let the student editors teach the newcomers the ropes. They take this assignment very seriously and after a few days, they pin their "graduate" in the class ceremony. Your goal is for every kid to become a graduate student editor by the end of the year. This system operates on the theory of limited access, and creates a desire for knowledge by linking it with prestige.

If for some reason training student editors would be impossible with your students, "borrow" a few older students from another classroom and make arrangements for them to help once a week or before school.

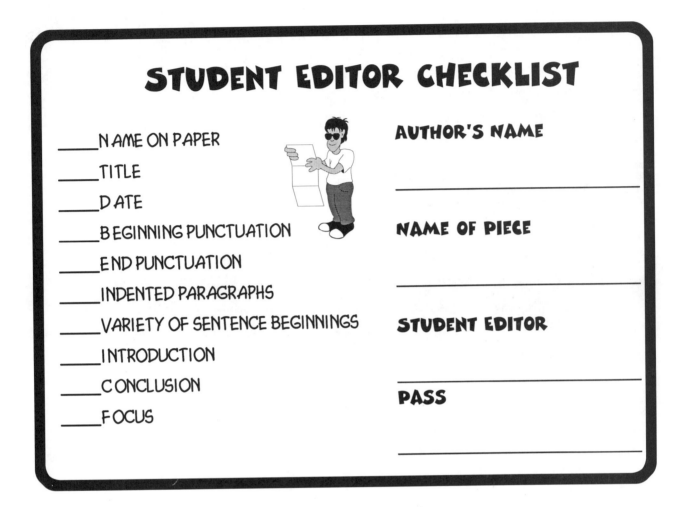

STUDENT EDITOR CHECKLIST

_____ NAME ON PAPER

_____ TITLE

_____ DATE

_____ BEGINNING PUNCTUATION

_____ END PUNCTUATION

_____ INDENTED PARAGRAPHS

_____ VARIETY OF SENTENCE BEGINNINGS

_____ INTRODUCTION

_____ CONCLUSION

_____ FOCUS

AUTHOR'S NAME

_____

NAME OF PIECE

_____

STUDENT EDITOR

_____

PASS

_____

Provide a "Pass" stamp or ask student editors to initial a checklist when everything has been successfully checked off. Change the checklist as you teach or emphasize new skills. The badge below fits in a standard plastic sleeve.

STUDENT EDITOR

_____

Has completed editorial training
for the 19__-19__ school year

Teacher _____

Small Group Benefits:

- ◆ **individual attention**
- ◆ **questions and answers**
- ◆ **increased discussion**
- ◆ **critical thinking**
- ◆ **focused attention**
- ◆ **more time on task**
- ◆ **modeling and examples**
- ◆ **increased self-confidence**
- ◆ **decreased vulnerability**
- ◆ **hands-on learning**
- ◆ **multiple learning styles**
- ◆ **repetition and practice**

GO!

The Daily Writing Workshop

Kids need an environment where they feel safe. Writing is an experience in vulnerability. Every writer needs the freedom to share his creative thoughts without the fear of being laughed at, scorned, or criticized by anyone. Kids often are asked for the right answer, but they are not often asked what they *think,* and writing begins with thinking.

A writing workshop is a good place to begin. Ask kids what they think about something, then wait. Be quiet. Thinking takes time. Encourage responses. Validate all participation. Endorse all original thoughts. For me, it is very satisfying to help students develop the ability to express themselves through writing. When they read, kids are learning valuable information from others, but when they write, they're contributing to the universal pool of knowledge. This concept is powerful and has a direct influence on academic success, future job opportunities, career choices, and self esteem. Your goal is to turn students into creative, accomplished, contributing authors.

How Do We Get To That Point?

- **Change what we've been doing.**
- **Relinquish total control.**
- **Break out of the traditional mold.**
- **Empower kids to become authors.**

By now, your students should have been exposed to a variety of genres and writing styles and will have a developing sense of what appeals to them. As discussed in Chapter 2, your writing-supply center will have an abundance of supplies available for kids to use. Each student will have a Self-Contained Writer's Notebook. You already will have taught writing skills in small groups and are now ready for the next step in classroom management, the Daily Writing Workshop.

Writing workshops work best early in the morning when brains are fresh. Vary the ambiance in the room. Experiment with many different forms of lighting: colored strings of lights, candles, unusual lamps, bright sunlight, a darkened room lit only by personal flashlights. Children relate the delicious feeling of special effects with the creative response of writing.

Try the effects of music on your writers: watch what happens when you play upbeat, galvanizing music, recordings of rain or songbirds, or the stimulating strains of an adventure movie soundtrack. My students look forward to each experience. Sometimes they're greeted by the scent of vanilla room spray, baking cookies, or melting chocolate. Popcorn assaults the ears and the nose! Creativity explodes!

Besides our regular writing centers and workshops, I try to lend variety to our environment by the occasional shift in location. A pretty day forecast for tomorrow might mean everyone brings a beach towel for an outside write-fest. We perch under trees, in the shade, around the flower beds—wherever we find sensory stimulation for descriptive writing.

Do you have a particular kid in your class who claims to hate writing? Get him to turn over a giant rock and write about all the creepy, wiggly creatures who suddenly appear. Bring a big magnifying glass for added fun. Ask kids to bring binoculars for revealing peeks up into the treetops. Challenge your writers to sniff stuff—all kinds of plants, dirt, moss, bugs, sticks, etc., and to describe the variety of different smells. Phew! Mmmmm!

Provide interesting items kids are not likely to have seen before. Hands-on observation and experimentation are two things all writers crave. An anticipatory hush falls over the room when I pull out a whale's tooth, giant rhinoceros beetle, stethoscope, treasure map, Miss America crown, skeleton, or an assortment of funny hats and costumes. I encourage kids to touch, try on, handle, observe, record, and most of all, experience.

Eyes widen. Gasps are heard. Brains go haywire.

Writing begins!

Structure must be present even in the midst of creativity and stimulation, as kids grow to depend on and anticipate a consistent writing time each day. Schedule your Daily Writing Workshop at a time when students are rested and able to think clearly. Allow few interruptions.

2nd grade.........30 minutes   3rd grade..........40 minutes

4th grade..........45 minutes   5th grade..........50 minutes

Each day the entire class participates in writing activities. I circulate, trouble-shoot, help, and praise. Whenever I teach a new concept or want to individualize my teaching, I go back to small groups for several days. Meeting the needs of individual writers is one strategy in developing a writing community.

How Does A Writing Workshop Work?

- Students and teachers come up with writing ideas.
- Students work at different writing centers around the room.
- Teacher circulates, encourages, and offers help.
- Students signal teacher when they need help.
- Students must be on-task at all times.
- Students are free to discuss and collaborate with peers.
- A signal indicates the noise level is too high for "thinking."
- Now and then someone announces the time.

Students Select Writing Topics

The ugly truth is out. Many teachers dread teaching writing or don't teach it often because they are intimidated by two things:
- having to select writing topics that will keep everyone happy
- having to grade writing*

Encouraging kids to come up with exciting, relevant writing topics shifts a whole lot of responsibility from the teacher to the student. The following script will help you visualize ways to steer students towards topics that will enhance units and themes you are teaching.

*addressed in Chapter 10

"LET'S STUDY MANATEES!"

A Writing Discussion Model

Teacher :	Gather round, my subjects. The great and mighty Queen has an announcement.
José :	Listen up, Ya'll.
DuBerry :	What is it, Mrs. Forney?
Teacher :	This is a class discussion, so I want to make sure everyone has input.
Shawna :	Hey, people! Pay attention.
Teacher :	As you know, we're just finishing the science unit on the rain forest. You guys did some great projects. It's time to switch gears, though. On Monday we'll be starting a new unit on manatees.
José :	Whoa! Cool!
Shawna :	Let her finish!
DuBerry :	I love animals. Manatees are my favorites.
Teacher :	Well, I know we're all interested in manatees because that topic has come up in a few of our discussions, right?
Class :	Yeah!
Teacher :	What are some ways we could find out information about manatees and present it to the class?
José :	I know. I could *draw* a manatee since I'm such a great artist.
Teacher :	We certainly need your skills, José. Would you draw a giant colored chart and label all the parts?
Tamara :	He could write a little paragraph about each part and what it...I mean...how it's useful to the manatee.
José :	My abuelita gave me new colored markers. They'll be perfect. Do you have a piece of paper that's big enough, Mrs. Forney?
Teacher :	I'll look for the perfect size this coming weekend. Let me know if you need a research pass to the media center to find information. I've got some magazines you can use, too.

DuBerry :	I know! My uncle used to work at Sea World. They had two manatees. I could call him.
Teacher :	A personal interview is an excellent way to get first-hand information. Why don't you prepare a list of important questions to ask, DuBerry?
Shemeeka :	Mrs. Forney, could I write a poem about manatees?
Teacher :	You have such a talent for poetry, Shemeeka. That's a nice idea. After you've written it, decide whether you would like to present it orally to the class or to make some sort of display with pictures.
Tamara :	Well, I love to write plays and do 'em for the class, but I don't really know how I could write a play about a manatee...
Teacher :	Anyone have any ideas?
Shawna :	I think you could do it, Tamara. My mom said that all the manatees have been dying. Some boats run over 'em and kill them, but some others are getting sick.
DuBerry :	They've had some sort of disease or something. Hey! What if you wrote it like some doctors and scientists trying to figure out how to help the manatees.
Tamara :	Yeah, before they all die off.
Teacher :	Do you two girls think you could work together to come up with a play?
Shawna :	Cool. Do you want to do that, Tam?
Tamara :	Yeah. That'd be better than just me.
Teacher :	Then the first step is for you to write a good script. It's got to be full of information to help the class learn all about manatees. Then, if you like, I'll help you stage it for the class.
José :	Could we *all* have a part?
Teacher :	I think you love acting as much as I do, José. Let's see what the girls come up with. Maybe we could do it as a class and present it to Mrs. Balfour's class.
DuBerry:	Oooo. That's a great idea!

47

Discussions like these are springboards for selecting writing topics for the entire year. Ownership is paramount. Students respond far better when they invest their own interests and enthusiasm into creative and informational writing. Good ideas lead to good writing.

How To "Grow" Ideas

Whenever ideas come to your students, ask them to write these down, no matter how offbeat or bizarre they might seem. Don't wait. They may use these years later or next week. Ask them to keep paper or sticky-notes by their beds, desks, in their cars, and in their backpacks or pockets. Keep pencils handy. When an idea strikes, they should write down at least some clue words as soon as possible. Kids can seize every opportunity for future stories by asking themselves: *How could this idea or experience be used in a story?* This is exactly how professional writers find and store ideas that they draw on throughout their writing careers. Almost every time I meet an interesting new person or hear a fascinating story, I mentally store it for some future article or story. A few of my best ideas came from kids!

Ideas Come From...

Personal experiences

Conversations

Stories we've been told

Interests

Our backgrounds

Daydreams

Characters

Triumphs/Defeats

Spin-offs of other ideas

Current issues

Emotions/Needs

Reading

Other people

When it comes to selecting writing topics, "ownership" is paramount!

CREATIVE WRITING SMORGASBORD

- Short Stories
- Fictionalized Interview
- Live Interview
- Phone Interview
- Puppet Play
- Choral Reading
- Classroom Play
- Video Drama
- "Soap Opera" Series
- Game for Back of Cereal Box
- Classroom Newspaper
- Poetry
- Illustrations and Text
- Picture Book
- Movie Script
- Letter to Celebrity
- Fictionalized Diary
- Time-Travel Description
- Personal Journal
- Advice Column
- Chapter Book
- Photography and Captions
- Shadow Box and Topper
- Hanging Rhyme List
- Rhyme Bank
- Name Bank
- First Line Bank
- Nursery Rhyme
- School Newsletter
- Suggestion Box

- "Concrete" Body Prose
- "Guess Who?" Biography
- Labels for Cans or Food Products
- Magnifying-Glass Description
- Radio Drama
- Hobby Description
- Job Description
- Topical Speech
- Slide Presentation/Voice Over
- Book Review
- Movie Review
- Restaurant Review
- Editorial for City Newspaper
- Current-Events Synopsis
- Daily or Weekly Weather Report
- Commercial
- Advertisement
- Cartoons/Comic Strip
- Helium-Balloon Message
- Phone Message
- Invitation
- Message in a Bottle
- "Progressive" Short Story
- Letter of Appreciation
- Pen Pal
- Newspaper Correspondent
- Secret Code
- Song Lyrics
- Thank-You Letter
- Letter of Complaint

Open-Ended Writing Assignments

Many teachers are used to giving a writing assignment, then allowing children time to write, revise, and proofread. Everyone works on the same assignment, a three-paragraph book report, and they're all due on the same date. This method assumes every student has the same learning style, attention span, and writing capabilities. I don't know about you, but I don't want to read 25 identical reports or listen to them read aloud in class. We'd hear identical information over and over. What's the solution?

The answer is open-ended assignments. As we discussed earlier, steer students in the direction of a theme or unit and encourage them to explore all manner of writing, the object being to find information and present it in a unique written format. Instead of 25 three-paragraph reports, your students might present book reports disguised as mock interviews, time-machine travel, poetry, songs, television commercials, with maybe a few traditional three-paragraph reports sprinkled in. This means not everyone will work on the same exact project or time frame. During two weeks of writing workshops, Candyce might complete one colossal project, Tyrone completes three or four smaller projects and Ken, five. All writing will be due in two weeks, but everyone's projects will be different.

During daily writing workshops kids will need to budget their time and plan what projects they will undertake and complete. The idea is for them to be on task every day, working towards completion within a certain period of time. Paula might write poetry today, put it away for three days, write a short report in the meantime, then come back to her poetry. Her responsibility is to have them accomplished within the given time frame. The structure of open-ended assignments encourages and enables students to practice individual responsibility.

Kids learn by the keen observation of others. Styles of dress, hair cuts, crazy fads—monkey see, monkey do. How can they learn about different levels of achievement if they are all required to accomplish the exact same things? With open-ended assignments you'll have some kids who fail to produce much at the beginning, and this is naturally somewhat disappointing to you as the teacher. But when these same kids see what others have produced in the same amount of time and the positive reinforcement they receive, it's an eye-opening experience.

For example, let's say Jason and Andrew make a model of the rain forest, complete with creeping vines and a menagerie of animals, to go with their report on Brazil. They have written and video taped a "news report" straight from the banks of the Amazon. A lot of time has been spent researching the information they used. Both boys have worked hard to make the accompanying video fun and informative.

The class goes wild! Your students absolutely love this kind of learning—it's fun and interesting. You praise Jason and Andrew and ask if you can show their work to Mrs. Maple's class. It doesn't take children long to want to produce the same kind of excellence. Other kids are already thinking *next time I'm going to do something cool like that!* It doesn't take a nagging teacher to prod children into becoming writers. Success, praise, encouragement, and enthusiasm do a much better job.

Help Is On The Way!

During the daily writing workshop, as mentioned before, it is important for the teacher to circulate among all students and give help as needed. It's good to establish a system for this early on so kids will stay on task even as they're waiting for you to help them. One reason open-ended assignments are a good idea is that writers can work on other assignments if they get "stuck" instead of sitting with their hands raised, wasting time.

Lynn Corombos, 3rd grade teacher, helps kids make laminated, construction paper hands, red on one side and green on the other, to signal her during writing workshop. If kids are on task, the hands stays green side up on their desks. If they need help, they turn up the red side so the teacher can stop while circulating through the room. You can also use construction paper traffic lights or "Help, please!" flags kids place on their desks. Another teacher, Jennifer Haller, wears an apron that contains extra pencils, pens, and rewards to have available as she circulates among her students.

Sample Point System

When first starting daily writing workshops, some teachers find their students function better with a set of guidelines to help set personal goals and fulfill responsibilities. Kids like cafeteria-style choices, and this is an excellent way to teach critical thinking, value judgements, and time budgeting. Feel free to adjust the "menu" to suit your classroom needs, to allow for other genres of writing, and to stress specific skills. Grading refers *only* to writing workshop grade.

WRITING WORKSHOP "MENU"

Entries in First Line bank - 1 point each (5 minimum)
Four character puppet play, two pages of dialogue - 15 points
One-page book review - 5 points
Short story with shadow box - 20 points
Letter to the editor, city newspaper - 10 points (+5 if published)
One-week historical diary - 10 points
Editing another writer's manuscript - 5 points
Rhyme Bank words - 1 point for every 5 words (5 minimum)
Completed rough-draft revision - 10 points
"Guess Who" interview and biography - 10 points
20-frame comic book and dialogue - 15 points
12-picture photo essay - 20 points
New vocabulary-word paragraph - 5 points
Pen-pal letter - 5 points
Original speech and presentation - 20 points
Reader critique of another writer's work - 5 points

POSSIBLE BONUS POINTS

Writer has been on task during daily writing workshops - 10 points
Exceptional creativity - 5 points
Exceptional citizenship - 5 points

POINT GRADING SYSTEM
(OPTIONAL—Please adapt to your needs! More about grading in Chapter 10)

90 - 120+ points = A
70 - 89 points = B
50 - 69 points = C
30 - 49 points = D   Points Earned: _____

Allow Writing to Rest

I almost always can spot a piece that has been written in one sitting. Writing improves as the author allows it to "rest" and looks at it again the next day. The new perspective spotlights repetitions, errors, poor word choice, and plot flaws. Train kids to look at their pieces several different times until there are no more errors to find.

Assignment Contracts

Some students seem to have responsibility born into them, while others have to be cajoled into completing the simplest of projects. Establishing a *writing assignment contract* is one way to get your kids to commit to a plan of action that will help keep them on task during the daily writing workshop. After studying the menu, brainstorming, and planning their courses of action, kids sign contracts, thereby committing to work on certain projects during a specified period of time.

Not all projects will come to completion. Kids like to try different styles, projects, and genres. This experimentation is fine as long as they focus in on some pieces to revise, edit, and publish.

ASSIGNMENT CONTRACT

Name_____ Date _____

My goal is to complete the following writing assignments:

_____

_____

_____

_____

_____

THE WRITING PROCESS

Five Easy Steps

The Writing Process is a term that refers to the five steps writers go through to create a work and bring it to completion.

STEP # 1	**PREWRITING**	**Planning before writing**
STEP # 2	**ROUGH DRAFT**	**Writing story/ideas down quickly**
STEP # 3	**REVISING**	**Making major changes to writing**
STEP # 4	**EDITING**	**Spelling, grammar, punctuation**
STEP # 5	**PUBLISHING**	**Sharing writing with readers**

STEP #1   PREWRITING

The planning stage of the writing process is almost more important to me than the actual writing. Many of the skills we use in our everyday lives such as cleaning, redecorating, or repairing require careful planning. Writing is no different. Planning makes the entire process enjoyable and rewarding. We call this planning "prewriting," and, as the name implies, it takes place before we begin writing. Some aspects of prewriting include:

- ★ **Thinking**
- ★ **Collecting Ideas**
- ★ **Brainstorming**
- ★ **Webbing**
- ★ **Storyboarding**
- ★ **Listening**
- ★ **Talking**
- ★ **Observation**

In the heat of a good idea, some students don't like to take the time to do prewriting, so they jump right into writing. It doesn't take long, however, for things to bog down or plot "holes" to become a problem. Prewriting is valuable because it helps writers:

- ▪ **Stay focused on the subject**
- ▪ **Think sequentially**
- ▪ **Form strategies for a beginning, middle and ending**
- ▪ **Come up with all options before writing**
- ▪ **Bounce ideas off other writers/consider suggestions**
- ▪ **Write descriptively**

Brainstorming

Brainstorming is a five-dollar word for listing. Students list as many ideas about a particular subject as they can think of, with no concern for any particular order or value judgement. When the list is exhausted, kids can cross out words that don't belong, re-group facts that go together, or get ideas of things they want to mention in their writing piece. This activity is great for class participation or can be done individually. Several good starting points for creative writing brainstorming are:

Setting: What are all the places the story could take place? Could you change the location to add interest?

Character: Who are the different characters that could be featured in your story? What is their personality like?

Subject: What are some subjects that interest you? Could you weave those into your story somehow?

Conflict: What kinds of problems could your characters face that would make the action more interesting?

Webbing

Webbing is an organized way for kids to arrange ideas, facts, and to plot details before beginning to write. Much like spiders weave webs, writers weave stories, detail by detail. Webbing keeps writers on track and headed in the right direction.

Start with the main idea in the center of the paper. Webbing outward, come up with as many subcategories as you can think of. You'll probably think of too many, but that's okay. Under each subcategory, write down details or bits of information that go with that topic. Now use the web to organize writing and remind you of important information.

As you refer back to the web, you can discard, change, or add additional information. As a creative alternative to traditional outlining, webbing gets our creative juices flowing and helps create intricate plots, detailed characters, and informative reports. Webbing is also a concrete checklist to help the writer remember key details that must be included.

Name_____   Date_____

BRAINSTORMING

Before you start to write, it's a good idea to brainstorm. This means coming up with as many ideas as you possibly can and listing them as fast as you think of them. For example, ice cream is a topic we all know something about. Think of a few more flavors to add to the list.

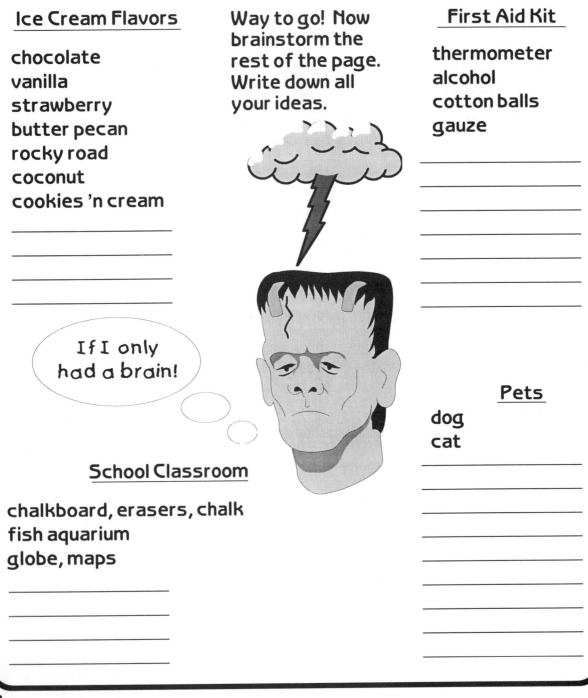

Ice Cream Flavors

chocolate
vanilla
strawberry
butter pecan
rocky road
coconut
cookies 'n cream

_____
_____
_____
_____

Way to go! Now brainstorm the rest of the page. Write down all your ideas.

If I only had a brain!

School Classroom

chalkboard, erasers, chalk
fish aquarium
globe, maps

_____
_____
_____
_____

First Aid Kit

thermometer
alcohol
cotton balls
gauze

_____
_____
_____
_____
_____

Pets

dog
cat

_____
_____
_____
_____
_____
_____

Reproducible exercise page

Name_____   Date_____

BRAINSTORMING CHARACTERS

Now that you've made several brainstorming lists, let's see if you can come up with some good details for characters you might write about in a story. For instance, just suppose you wanted to write a story about a boy, Eddie, who catches some bank robbers during a parade.

What would he look like? How old would he be? What are some of the things he likes to do? What is his home life like? What other details could you tell the reader that would make the "Eddie" character believable? Here is an example of how you can brainstorm by character:

His name is Eddie Bumfuzzle
red hair, freckles, 11 years old
skinned knee, skateboard wreck
likes to solve scary mysteries
has three best friends, all guys
has a secret tree house
loves excitement and adventure
lives with his grandmother
eats chocolate candy bars
skinny, tall, athletic
very funny, loves to tell jokes
always exaggerates the truth!

Can't you just picture him in your mind? He would be easy to write about now because we have a list of details.

Your turn! Brainstorm one of Eddie's best friends. Create as many details as you can so that we feel like we know this person. Be sure to make him different from Eddie!

Name_____   Date_____

We can use brainstorming to help us come up with story ideas before we write. Sometimes kids say, "I don't know what to write about." Brainstorm a few story ideas and keep them in your Idea Bank. Here are a few starters. Each idea could be developed into a story.

B R A I N S T O R M I N G

A Teacher who...
takes her class on a canoe trip
forgets to wear shoes to school
dyes her hair purple
runs away with the circus
throws a surprise party for the principal
finds gold hidden in the classroom piano
brings banana and onion sandwiches for lunch

Have I got a story for you!

A Dog Who...
got a bone stuck in his throat
stole your family's meatloaf
rescues a little girl from a snake
rips a hole in your school costume
eats some magic dog biscuits
talks to the girl who owns him

A Kid Who...
beats up other kids after school
wins a prize for saving someone's life
eats so many tomatoes he turns red
has a magic carpet
brings octopus cookies to class
loses her mother's wedding ring
teachers his baby brother to read
babysits for a very rich family
goes camping with the principal's family
has a crush on his best friend's sister

58

Name_____ Date_____

W E B B I N G

Did you ever watch a spider spin its web? Little by little it spins different parts of the web until it's strong and useful. You can web, too, before you write, and your story or paragraph will be organized and easier to keep on track. Webbing is easy! Just start with a main idea, and spin off other little ideas.

Let's say your subject is cars. That's a big subject, right? You know so much information about cars, where would you begin?

Begin by putting the main idea, cars, in the center of your paper. Then spin off other smaller ideas out from the center. Draw boxes or circles around your ideas. This way you can break down all of the information you know about cars into different topics and choose one to write about.

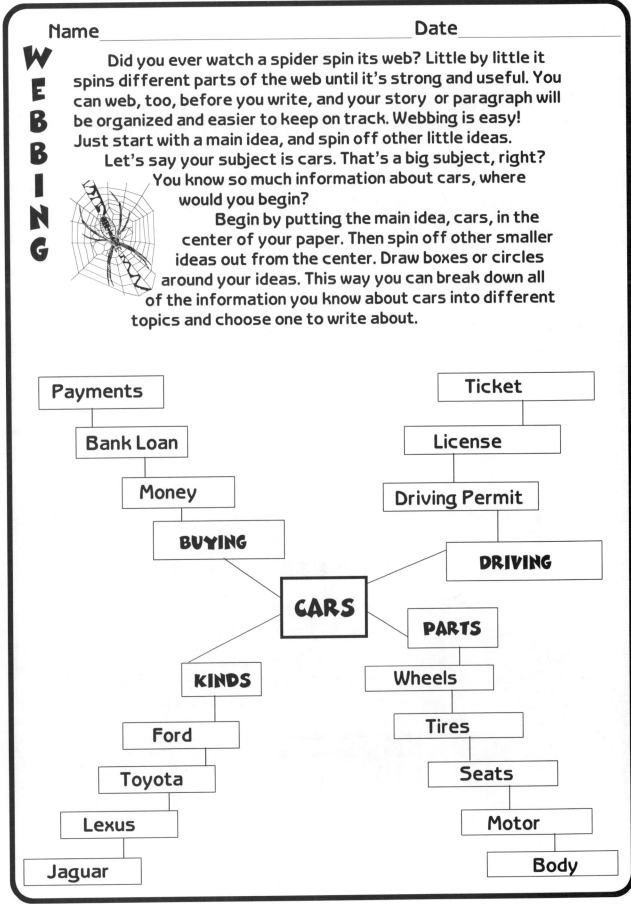

Payments
Bank Loan
Money
BUYING

Ticket
License
Driving Permit
DRIVING

CARS

KINDS
Ford
Toyota
Lexus
Jaguar

PARTS
Wheels
Tires
Seats
Motor
Body

Reproducible exercise page

59

Name_____ Date_____

Try webbing. Your topic will be....the USA! What a huge topic. You know a lot of things about the United States of America. First, organize some of the information you know into different parts of a web. Web from the center out. Try to list things that go together, such as states, counties, cities, and towns. If you need more boxes, draw them yourself. When you finish, share your web with the rest of the students in your class.

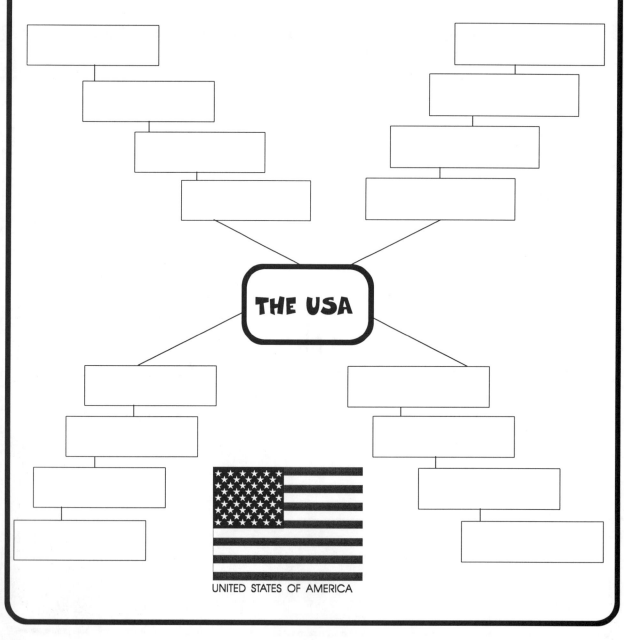

UNITED STATES OF AMERICA

Sequencing With Storyboards

Once you hit on a great idea for a story, getting it in the right sequence is a helpful step. This is where the storyboard comes in. Television and movie makers use this method to create intricate stories, and the same strategy works great for kids, too.

Fold sheets of paper, work with a printed grid, or use sticky-notes. After you've brainstormed, webbed, or outlined, put your basic story plot in storyboard form. That way you can move things around and change them if necessary. Some writers change their storyboards even during the writing process, especially when they have a complicated plot. Writers love to make changes!

Teach kids to use simple stick figures to quickly portray character movement and plot details. The following frames are the beginning storyboard of a story about a boy who always loses his glasses:

1 — Tim - glasses	2 — Broke, lost	3 — Hid glasses under bush
4 — Wrong house	5 — Ran home	6 — Glasses gone!

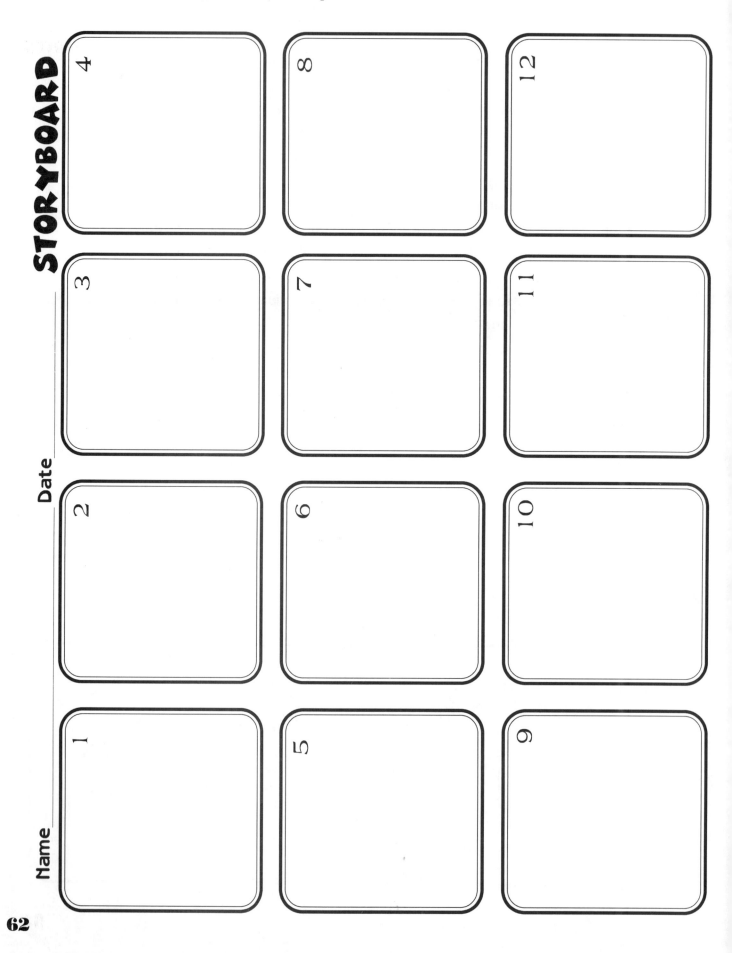

STORYBOARD

Date

Name

STEP #2   ROUGH DRAFT

I wish I had a nickel for every writer who tried to write a final draft on the first go-round. Brains are funny things. They spew out thoughts and ideas quickly in a burst of creativity, and we've got to write them down before they disappear. The first time we do this is called a rough draft, because it's a rough sketch of the final picture.

Do me a favor—don't call this a *sloppy copy*! It rhymes but it doesn't describe what we're trying to get kids to do. I'm not obsessed with neatness but I don't want to promote sloppiness either. The proper term is rough draft, and it's important for kids to use the terms real authors use.

First of all, have kids write on greenbar paper, the green and white striped paper usually used by bank computer printers. It's marvelous for writing because it automatically reminds kids to skip lines. It's a proven fact that kids' writing improves when they skip lines because they have room for revisions and don't have to copy over unless they're going to publish. This strategy drastically changed the way I teach writing.

Next, be sure authors are not interrupted while writing rough drafts. Supersonic ideas are hard to come by, and once they're lost, there's not a whole lot you can do about it. Kids should have lots of blank greenbar paper in their notebooks so they don't have to get up for more while writing rough drafts.

I use these reminders when guiding young writers through the rough draft process:

- **Define your purpose for writing.**
- **Know your audience.**
- **Stay focused on your topic.**
- **Write down thoughts, ideas, or plot quickly.**
- **Use temporary spelling and circle it as you write.**
- **Don't worry about using the dictionary at this point.**
- **Get as much written down as you can.**
- **Stop just before you get to the solution of the plot.**
- **Write the solution of the plot on another day.**

Name_____ Date_____

STAY FOCUSED!

Good writers keep focused on their topic. *Focus* means all sentences should have something to do with the main idea of the paragraph. Can you tell when a writer has not stayed focused? Read the paragraphs below. Underline the sentences that should be taken out because they are not focused on the main idea of the paragraph.

A DAY AT THE BEACH

Last weekend my family went to the beach. The weather was perfect. My sister and I swam even though the water was cold. It gets cold in Indiana where my grandmother lives. We rode the waves on our air mattresses. My mother brought a picnic lunch, so we ate on an old blanket and tried not to get sand on our fried chicken. Boy, were we hungry! I get hungry at school, too. After lunch we walked down the beach looking for shells. I found a lot of sand dollars and a live starfish. At 4:00 my mother said it was time to go. We helped her load all our stuff in the car and then headed home. I like to sit in the front seat. Even though I got sunburned we still had a great day at the beach.

PEANUT BUTTER AND JELLY

One of my favorite sandwiches is peanut butter and jelly. I take one to school for lunch every day. We eat in the cafeteria. Peanut butter is good for you. My friend Joshua brings ham and cheese. First, you spread some peanut butter on a piece of bread. You can use smooth peanut butter or crunchy. Then you spread your favorite kind of jelly on another piece of bread and put the two pieces together. Peanut butter and jelly goes well with cold milk to drink. No wonder so many kids love peanut butter and jelly sandwiches for snacks or lunch. They're easy to make and so delicious!

Were you a good detective? Three sentences in the first paragraph were not focused. Two sentences in the second paragraph were not focused.

Name_____ Date_____

CAN YOU STAY FOCUSED?

Now it's your turn. Write four sentences about dogs. Make sure the information you write is just about dogs and doesn't stray off the topic.

_____

_____

_____

_____

Read your sentences aloud to your partner. Check *Yes* if all your sentences were about dogs and *No* if at least one sentences was not.

_____ Yes   _____ No

This time write four or five sentences to make a short paragraph about your bedroom. Describe your room and tell what you do there. Make sure every sentence is about the topic of your bedroom. Stay focused!

_____

_____

_____

_____

_____

When you and your partner have finished, read each other's paragraphs. Look for any sentences that are not focused. Improve them, if you need to. Now take turns reading your paragraphs aloud to the class.

STEP #3   REVISING

An ugly baby is always beautiful to its mother, and most writers think their manuscripts are perfect after one draft. A mistake some kids make is to assume they're finished after the rough draft stage. *I'm done! What next?* They never experience improving their work, which we call **revising.** Revising is a crucial step, and helps us mature as writers. Without it, we always remain in the baby stage—the ugly baby stage, that is. While some pieces will remain as drafts, others must be revised.

Kids don't mind revising nearly as much if they write on greenbar paper, skip lines, and have plenty of room to add or correct. Overcrowding leads to frustration. After the rough draft is written, the author should read the piece aloud. For some reason, we catch errors and omissions when our ears hear them aloud *better* than when we skim over them with our eyes. Peer-conferencing is an important step in revising. It's always good to have readers respond to what we have written, ask questions, and make suggestions. Teacher Jane Willingham makes colorful "baloney sandwiches" for her students. When an author reads her rough draft to the class, they hold up the "bread" side for a compliment and the "baloney" side for advice or a suggestion. The author then makes a "sandwich" by calling for one "bread," one "baloney" and another "bread."

The next step is to make changes on the original rough draft by writing between the lines of original text. My students write in pencil and revise in colored ink so I can *see* how much revision has been done.

Kids are always surprised to learn that writers revise their books as many as 30 or more times. Keep at it until you have a masterpiece! Anyone can write a lot of stories, but few hone them to perfection.

Don't copy over. Don't copy over! Did I mention: Don't copy over!? We are not concerned with neatness and perfect margins at this stage. Temporary spelling is fine for the moment. Right now we are concerned only with content, clarity, details, description. Is it a terrific story? Do you make me laugh? Is the ending powerful? Does the report tell me all I want to know about tarantulas? Does the poem allow me to feel your pain? Can I relate to the main character? Does the dialogue sound real? Is there any part I can't understand?

PEER-CONFERENCE QUESTIONS

———— Do I know who the main characters are and something about them?

———— Do I know where the story takes place?

———— Is the conflict (problem) clear?

———— Does the writer use words that make me see, hear, taste, feel, and smell?

———— Does the conflict have a satisfying solution?

———— Does the writer end with a conclusion? (ending)

The part I like best is ————————————————————————

——

One idea you might try is ————————————————————

Signed,————————————————————————

STEP #4   EDITING

Editing is the step in writing that makes our work presentable to others and gets it ready for publication. Up until this point, we haven't concerned ourselves too much with margins, neatness, and final form. Now is the time to check grammar, punctuation, and capitalization and to correct temporary spelling.

A word about temporary spelling: It's perfectly acceptable during the writing process. Temporary spelling is like a spare tire—good for short-term but it won't take you all the way to New Orleans. As kids write rough drafts, they circle words they aren't sure how to spell. During the editing process they will look these words up in the dictionary, word speller, unit list, or vocabulary-word list, and make corrections.

After editing their pieces, students then present them to student editors for a final check before filing them in their Self-Contained Writer's Notebooks or submitting them to the teacher during an assessment appointment. If the rough draft is neat enough to read, even with corrections, it shouldn't be copied over unless it's going to be published.

STEP #5   PUBLISHING

Publishing is the celebration of a completed work and, like writing, manifests itself in many ways. Authors can add illustrations, make books, give dramatic presentations or speeches, read aloud, share from the Author's Chair, or any number of other creative ideas. Chapter 11 will deal extensively with publishing.

As mentioned before, not all works will get to the publishing stage. Lots and lots of writing will take place in your classroom and it would be impossible for an author to publish every idea or story he writes about. Careful consideration must be given to choose pieces for publication.

The Benefits Of Process Writing

In an effort to assess the writing skills of American school children, many states have adopted a state writing-assessment test. The information gathered from these tests clearly indicates students who have a strong background in process writing consistently do well. The five steps of the writing process are important to a writer's development and improve assessment scores.

The mastery of the writing process also provides kids with:

* **sequential steps to follow**

* **critical thinking skills**

* **the ability to plan**

* **an interchange of ideas with peers**

* **confidence to expresss themselves through writing**

* **a foundation for revising and improving their work**

* **the experience of having their writing published**

Temporary spelling is kind of like a spare tire—good for short-term, but it won't take you all the way to New Orleans!

Writing Workshop Reminders...

- Writing is a thought process.
- Students respond to a variety of teaching strategies.
- Each child is an individual.
- Divide and conquer!
- Writing centers stimulate different learning styles.
- Most children can communicate well verbally.
- Illustrating is only one form of writing enhancement.
- Identify each skill you want to teach.
- Use kids to teach other kids.
- Expose kids to many different genres of writing.
- Model everything many times!
- Use Self-Contained Writer's Notebooks for all writing.
- Use highlighters to reinforce sight words or content words.
- Train kids to give and receive compliments.
- Train kids to give and receive constructive criticism.
- Demonstrate and emphasize the permanency of writing.
- Provide many choices of writing projects.
- Emphasize staying on task.
- Utilize home time for thinking, writing, and reader/response.
- Train parents! For goodness sake, TRAIN PARENTS!
- Every writer should be familiar with the writing process.
- All writing is meant to be read or shared.
- Allow kids time to think and organize their thoughts.
- Not all writing will be brought to closure.
- Empower kids to take responsibility for some choices.
- Thoughtless comments can stifle a kid's creativity forever!
- Box and share writing props with other teachers.
- Writing and writing time should be *ongoing.*
- Never underestimate the life-changing power of praise.
- Every masterpiece can be traced back to a teacher.

NARRATIVES
Writing Stories

Children grow up learning to love stories, or **narratives**. Since birth they've listened to stories, verbal accounts, and recordings; they've gone to the movies, watched videos, and hours of television. Stories are an integral part of their language development and cultural reference point. All kids beg, "Tell me a story!"

There's some debate on this point, but I'm on the side of those who believe avid readers make good writers. From my own experience, I've seen that proven true many times. Reading subconsciously familiarizes kids with plot devices, character development, dialogue, and voice. This helps children develop an "ear" for the cadence and rhythm of writing.

Fact Or Fiction?

Kids sometimes get the mistaken notion that narratives are fiction and expository writing is factual. Not so! Both can be fiction or factual. For instance, your friend might tell you about the time she was robbed while sight-seeing in Paris. She relates the story from beginning to end, describing events that really happened. This is a narrative. Someone else might make up a story to top hers, but it is purely imaginative. This is also a narrative. What defines a narrative? Narrative writing shows the passage of time. Certain events, real or imaginary, take place in a sequenced order, and are related in an engrossing, mesmerizing way.

The Creative Writing Story Balloon, on the following page, is a graphic way to teach kids the basic components of the narrative and can be used as an overhead. The answers are detailed on page 71.

As your writers mature, be sure to showcase other genres of narratives: dramas, puppet plays, chapter books, comic books, etc. Well written narratives make us care about characters and involve our emotions, senses, and imaginations. The writer reinvents the world as he wants it to be, weaves a plot, and takes the reader with him on an unforgettable journey.

Name_____ Date_____

THE CREATIVE WRITING STORY BALLOON

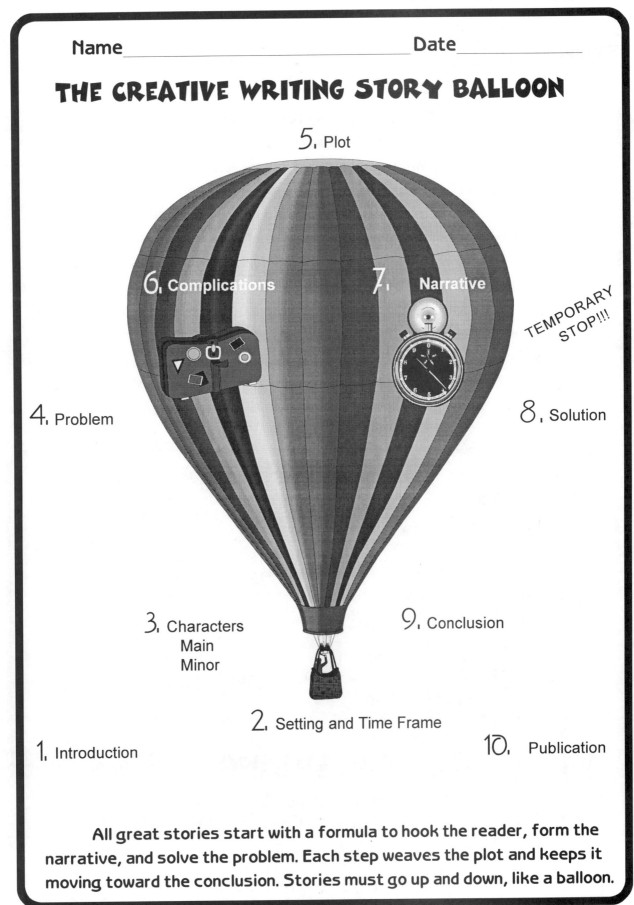

5. Plot

6. Complications   7. Narrative

TEMPORARY STOP!!!

4. Problem   8. Solution

3. Characters
Main
Minor

9. Conclusion

2. Setting and Time Frame

1. Introduction   10. Publication

All great stories start with a formula to hook the reader, form the narrative, and solve the problem. Each step weaves the plot and keeps it moving toward the conclusion. Stories must go up and down, like a balloon.

ANSWERS
THE CREATIVE WRITING STORY BALLOON

1. Introduction - Hooks the reader by creating interest
2. Setting and Time Frame - Tell when and where the story takes place
3. Characters - Tell who the story is about

    Main characters have names, physical details, personalities

    Minor characters have functions
4. Problem - Makes the story action rise
5. Plot - The storyline
6. Complications - Unexpected things must happen to the characters
7. Narrative - Must show the passing of time

    Temporary Stop!! - Writers write a better solution at another sitting
8. Solution - Solves the problem and satisfies the reader
9. Conclusion - Finished the story to the very end. Never write The End!
10. Publication - Establishes a relationship between author and reader

STORY QUESTIONS

BEGINNING

How will I hook my reader?
Who is my main character?
Where does the story take place?
When does the story take place?

MIDDLE

What is the problem?
How is the main character involved?
What happens next?
What happens after that?

ENDING

How is the problem solved?
What happens to the main character?
How does he feel?
What does he learn?
How do I satisfy my reader?

Name_____ Date_____

STORY PLANNER

SETTING (WHERE?)

TIME (WHEN?)

MAIN CHARACTER'S NAME, PHYSICAL DESCRIPTION, PERSONALITY DETAILS

OTHER CHARACTERS

STORY PROBLEM DETAILS

SOLUTION DETAILS

HOOK (OPENING SENTENCE)

Name_____   Date_____

DESCRIPTIVE WRITING

Who wants to read something boring? When you read a scary story, don't you want to know the juicy details? People like to picture things in their own minds. The answer is for you to give clues, details, and specific descriptions of things you write about. Let's see if we can figure out how to make our writing more descriptive. Think of your senses: sight, smell, hearing, taste and touch. List 10 words that fit those categories. A few clues will help you get started.

SIGHT	SMELL	HEARING	TASTE	TOUCH
blue	stinky	buzzing	bitter	velvety
little	chocolatey	crunch	salty	smooth
blurry	perfumy	whisper	tangy	rough
round	rotten	snap	metallic	slippery
1.	1.	1.	1.	1.
2.	2.	2.	2.	2.
3.	3.	3.	3.	3.
4.	4.	4.	4.	4.
5.	5.	5.	5.	5.
6.	6.	6.	6.	6.
7.	7.	7.	7.	7.
8.	8.	8.	8.	8.
9.	9.	9.	9.	9.
10.	10.	10.	10.	10.

"These worms are delicious. I especially like their slimy skin!"

Name_____ Date_____

Read the paragraph below. It is very descriptive, don't you think? After you read it through, go back and underline the words that actually helped you taste, feel, see, hear, and smell. These are descriptive words.

Take Your Medicine!

My mother told me in a stern voice that I would have to take medicine. How I hated that! The last time she made me take medicine it was supposed to be cherry flavored but it was bitter. I still remember how the thick syrup coated my tongue with a horrible taste. I shut my eyes, trying to avoid it. But I could hear the flip of the bottle's lid and the clink of the spoon as she poured it out. "Open up," she said, placing the small, brown bottle back on the table. What a surprise! The medicine was not bitter or sour. It was kind of sweet and tasted like bananas. Afterwards, I drank a small glass of cool water. Taking medicine wasn't so bad after all.

Describe the meal you ate for supper last night. Be sure to use words that paint a clear picture in the reader's mind. When you are through, read your paragraph aloud.

_____

_____

_____

_____

_____

_____

_____

_____

Name_____ Date_____

CHECKLIST FOR NARRATIVES

Anyone can write, but an author keeps
polishing until a piece is ready to publish.
You can create a masterpiece!

Show, don't tell.

Stimulate the reader's imagination.

Write dialogue the way people talk.

Know your audience.

Hook the reader right away.

Know your characters well and describe them to your reader.

Describe both good and bad characteristics.

Use strong nouns and verbs.

Avoid using too many adjectives and adverbs.

Stay in the same narrative voice and verb tense.

Keep sentences to less than 15 words.

Write the first sentence and title last.

Use five or less words in your title. Start each word with a capital letter.

Write like you talk. Informal "kid" vocabulary is best.

Get your rough draft down as quickly as you can!

Don't use the same word twice in a sentence or paragraph.

Vary the beginnings of your sentences.

Keep going back to the beginning and read what you've written.

Read your work silently and then aloud to find your own mistakes.

Don't read your work to others until you've finished the rough draft.

Remember, writing takes a lot of time.

Congratulate yourself after each writing session.

Begin each writing session by rereading your manuscript.

Write the solution to the problem on a second day.

Allow your manuscript "to rest" for a few days.

Read and respond; ask several other writers to read and critique.

Revise...revise...revise! A finished work requires many drafts.

Read and respond again. Read with a critical eye for improvement.

Write your final draft. Print out and edit it carefully. Allow it to rest, edit again.

Proofread. Spellcheck. Word count. Illustrate.

Have a student editor check and proofread.

You are ready to publish!

Reproducible exercise page

Name_____ Date_____

SENTENCE COMBINING

Do you remember when you first started to write paragraphs and stories? Chances are, most of your sentences were short, like these:

Baseball is a sport. It is fun. I play baseball with my brother. His name is Tom.

As you mature as a writer you learn to combine sentences together. This way you can give more information in one sentence. For instance, all of the information in the baseball sentences could be combined into one meaningful sentence:

My brother Tom and I have fun playing the sport of baseball.

Isn't that neat? Sentence combining makes sense. When you give more information in one sentence, instead of four, it makes your writing more mature. Try combining these sentences:

Susan is going to the movie. Allison is going with her. The girls are best friends. The movie is on Saturday.

_____

_____

How did you do? Sentence combining makes your paragraphs and stories easier to read and understand, too. Try one more:

The pizza was covered with pepperoni. It was delicious. It had lots of cheese. I bought it at Pizza Hut. I bought it yesterday.

_____

_____

There are several ways to combine these sentences. Did you include all of the information? If so, you are becoming a mature writer!

Name_____ Date_____

Underline the sentences that can be combined. Don't overload!

SATURDAYS

On Saturday mornings, I like to sleep late. I never set my alarm clock. I wake up about 10:00 usually. My mom cooks breakfast. She cooks breakfast every Saturday. She cooks my favorite breakfast. My favorite breakfast is pancakes, bacon, grits, and eggs. After breakfast, I help clean the house. I clean for about an hour. Then I have the rest of the day. During the rest of the day, I play. Sometimes I play outside with my friends. Sometimes I go to the mall. I like Saturdays. I can do what I want to.

If you have a good eye, you underlined several sentences that can be combined. Now rewrite the paragraph on the lines below. Combine sentences and make sure the reader will get all the information.

_____

_____

_____

_____

_____

_____

_____

You kids are very creative, so there might be several different ways to combine these sentences into a dense, mature paragraph. Take turns reading yours with a partner or in groups. Now when you write paragraphs and stories, be sure to *go back and see if any of your sentences can be combined!* If they can, revise so that your sentences are full of information.

Narrative Writing Practice Prompts

It almost kills me to get kids ready for a state writing assessment test, but I'm called on to do it all the time. Everything in me screams out against it. Stringent rules and time constraints are the antithesis of what I believe are good writing criteria. The pressure is on to assess student writing, so many teachers must spend a great deal of time preparing kids for the test. This leaves little time for natural, spontaneous, creative writing. However, prepare we must. Here are some examples to help kids practice writing to a given prompt.

Everyone has lost something important before.
   A. Before you begin writing, think about something you have lost.
   B. Try to remember the details of how you felt and what you did.
   C. Now tell about the time you lost something important, using words that will make the reader feel, hear, see, and experience what happened in your story.

Imagine what happens if you are accidentally locked in your school overnight and no one knows you are there. You are all alone!
   A. Think of some of the feelings you might have as soon as you realize you are locked in and at different times during the night.
   B. Imagine some of the events that happen to you.
   C. Now tell the story using descriptive language, so the reader can picture and experience what happens on the night you spend accidentally locked in your school.

One day you're on your way home from school and you find a strange looking box hidden under a bush. You decide to see what's inside.
   A. Think of the details of how you find the box.
   B. Think of what is in the box when you open the lid.
   C. Now tell the story of finding the box and, using words, action, and dialogue, describe exactly what happens.

Imagine your grandmother asks you to keep her parakeet while she goes on vacation. This sounds like a simple assignment, but some unusual things happen while you are keeping the parakeet. What an experience!
   A. Before you begin writing, think of some things that can happen.
   B. List some adventures and problems and describe your reactions.
   C. Now tell the story of keeping your grandmother's parakeet.

You come home from school and find the front door of your house is wide open. Things inside look really messed up. You've been robbed!
   A. Think of some of the feelings you might have.
   B. List the things you should do in this situation.
   C. Now tell the story in an exciting way.

9 EXPOSITORY WRITING

Writing To Explain

Expository writing is explanatory communication based on supportive facts or reasons. Kids already use expository skills such as sharing an opinion, giving directions, or explaining why they got dirty at recess. Harnassing these skills and teaching students to support their opinions and explanations with specific details or reasons is our goal.

As with narrative writing, expository writing can be fiction or nonfiction, depending on whether the facts it is based on are true or untrue. The key is that all expository writing must be supported by reasons, details, definitions, directions, or arguments.

Did you ever wonder why when kids take a writing-assessment test, they seem to do better on narrative writing than on expository? It's my theory that while they frequently use oral expository skills, they've had more practice writing narratives. From the time kids first enter school they are asked to tell or write stories and illustrate with crayons or markers. They associate writing with drawing, which they enjoy. Emerging writers might not write opinion pieces, recipes, directions, or persuasive pieces because these things are more difficult to illustrate with drawings. Another theory is that kids need to be asked more frequently to give their opinions and to explain information with specific details.

Kids respond well when they know what is expected of them. After learning a few helpful formulas they write wonderful expository pieces. The good news is kids who have mastered these formulas have greatly improved their expository skills and test scores. The same good writing techniques they learn in your classroom will be of value throughout their college education, careers, and personal lives.

All expository writing must be supported by reasons, details, directions, or arguments.

The Importance of Expository Writing

We live in a world of communication, much of it written. As more and more information is passed via computers, the Internet and fax machines, it is crucially important to be a master of good writing skills. During the near future, your students will be called on to communicate in virtual reality, without the benefit of personality or body language. They will be "known" by the tenor and expertise of their writing skills.

Since expository writing is explanatory in nature, it involves the imparting of knowledge, a responsibility kids must become aware of and accept in order to see themselves as authors. Students will use expository writing to add to the common knowledge pool both now, in your classroom, and as they go through life. Therefore, it is extremely important for them to become familiar with and be able to write in many different formats and genres of expository writing.

Help your students start a classroom collection of different types of expository writing and discuss its impact on our society. Children write eagerly when they believe in the purpose and value of what they're doing. Utilize every opportunity to foster "real" writing that will be used, mailed, published, produced, read, received, followed, printed, presented or sung. After your students get excited about the importance of exposition, they'll never again ask you, "Will we ever need this stuff?"

EXPOSITORY WRITING? YOU'RE KIDDING!

Instruction	Opinion
"How To"	Editorials
Recipes	Recommendations
Rules	Book Reviews
Directions	Movie Reviews
Planning	Critiques
Information	Poetry
Essays	Comparisons
Biographies	Advice Columns
Autobiographies	Suggestions
Research Papers	**Persuasion**
Current Events	Debates
Letters	Rebuttals
Summaries	Letters of Complaint
Paraphrases	Courtroom Strategies
Comparisons	Challenges
Invitations	Speeches
Announcements	Arguments
Reports	Political Campaigns
Journalism	Personal Convictions
Observations	Advertisements
Poetry	Commands
Song Lyrics	Dialogue

81

Name_____   Date_____

HOW IN THE WORLD DO YOU "RESTATE" SOMETHING?

In expository writing you're going to see the term "restate" quite often. To "state" means to tell something, so to "restate" means to tell it again. Restating reminds the reader what you think is important. When we restate something we write it a little differently or put it another way so we won't be repeating the exact same words. Read the examples below:

State: Most kids enjoy playing video games with their friends.

Restate: Playing video games is a good way to have fun with your buddies.

State: Watching a horror movie scares the living daylights out of me!

Restate: If I ever want to be frightened out of my wits, all I have to do is watch a scary movie!

Now you try. Restate the following sentences in a different way. Remember to change the beginning of your sentences, too. Take turns reading them aloud to the rest of the class. They'll all be different! That's what makes writing interesting.

State: My grandfather was one of the best fishermen around.

Restate: _____

_____

State: Lots of people think snakes are creepy, but I think they're neat.

Restate: _____

_____

State: I hate having to do homework when I've been in school all day.

Restate: _____

_____

State: It takes a lot of hard work to become an Olympic athlete.

Restate: _____

_____

State: Junk food isn't really good for you but it sure does taste great.

Restate: _____

_____

"How To" Paragraph

Want to learn how to skydive?

One of the most basic forms of expository writing is the "how to" paragraph. Your students can use the prewriting planner and help sheets that follow. Here are some tips for well-written, "how to" paragraphs:

★ **Use the title to "tease" your readers.**

★ **Use five words or less in the title.**

★ **Don't include "How To" in the title. That's too obvious!**

★ **Make sure your topic sentence clearly states your topic.**

★ **List all important steps from beginning to end.**

★ **Use transition words.**

★ **Vary sentence beginnings.**

★ **Restate the topic sentence at the end of the paragraph.**

"HOW TO" PARAGRAPH FORMULA

TOPIC_____

TOPIC SENTENCE_____

_____

STEP 1 _____

STEP 2 _____

STEP 3 _____

STEP 4 _____

STEP 5 _____

STEP 6 _____

STEP 7 _____

STEP 8 _____

RESTATE TOPIC SENTENCE_____

_____

Name_____ Date_____

TRANSITION WORDS

Transition Words are like little bridges that take us smoothly from idea to idea. They make the steps of a "how to" paragraph easier to understand.

Here are some transition words:

To begin
First of all
The first step is
For example
Another example
At this point
For instance
In particular
Also
However
Though
On the other hand
Furthermore
As a result
Consequently
To start off
In the beginning
Before
After
After that step
Later
In a little while
Next
The next step
Then
Now
When
First
Second
Third
Last
Finally
In conclusion
At last

Circle all the transition words in this "how to" paragraph.

Five-Minute Ice Cream

When kids get home in the afternoon, they are always hungry and looking for good snacks. Five-minute ice cream is easy for kids to make and delicious, too. To begin, gather your stuff. You'll need a medium and a large resealable plastic bag. First, pour two tablespoons of sugar into the medium-size bag. Then pour in one cup of milk. Next, add one teaspoon of vanilla flavoring. Carefully seal the bag shut and put it inside the large bag. Now put a bunch of ice cubes in the big bag all around the medium bag. You'll need several handfuls of ice. Sprinkle six or seven tablespoons of regular salt over the ice cubes. Next, seal the big bag and place it in a pillow case or wrap it in a towel. It's ready to freeze! Shake the bag for five minutes while the ice cream freezes, then rinse the middle size bag off very quickly under cold water. At last, the ice cream is ready to eat. Spoon it into some cups, pass out spoons, and enjoy. Delicious! Homemade ice cream hits the spot. The next time someone asks, "What's for snack?", try this recipe for five-minute ice cream.

The Five-Paragraph Essay

After students learn to write well-structured paragraphs, the next step is to teach the five-paragraph essay. *Five paragraphs!* I used to say. *Not my students!* Now after teaching this method to thousands of children, I've watched reluctant writers expand their writing from a few sentences into beautiful, five-paragraph essays.

The five-paragraph essay, well-supported by details, is the form of expository writing that helps students do well on writing-assessment tests. Scorers are usually looking for an organizational plan, valid reasons, or arguments supported by specific details and examples.

Take it step by step. I help kids memorize the formula first and then spend one writing workshop on each paragraph until my students have written a complete five-paragraph essay. After modeling this process several times, I find students are able to come up with logical, weighty, supporting arguments on their own. What a breakthrough! Mastering this formula gives kids the confidence they need to express themselves through expository writing and to score well on assessment tests.

THE FIVE-PARAGRAPH ESSAY FORMULA

FIRST PARAGRAPH	=	Introduction Main Topic Sentence Three Main Reasons (Or ideas)
SECOND PARAGRAPH	=	Main Reason #1 (Topic Sentence) Specific Details and Examples
THIRD PARAGRAPH	=	Main Reason #2 (Topic Sentence) Specific Details and Examples
FOURTH PARAGRAPH	=	Main Reason #3 (Topic Sentence) Specific Details and Examples
FIFTH PARAGRAPH	=	Restate Main Topic Sentence Restate Three Main Reasons Conclusion

Name_____   Date_____

THE FIVE PARAGRAPH ESSAY

Read this five-paragraph essay, written by a kid. Each paragraph is numbered. The main topic sentence is underlined. The three main reasons are underlined twice. Keep this as an example to help you follow the formula.

Goosebumps From *Goosebumps*!

Introduction

#1   Everyone knows that reading is good for us. Kids like to read all sorts of stuff. We even read the back of the cereal box. Moms make us read homework, teachers make us read textbooks, and coaches make

Topic Sentence

3 Main Reasons

us read the plays of the game. But lots of kids will agree, R.L. Stine's *Goosebumps* series is the most fun for us to read. The books are educational, scary, and very entertaining.

One reason, specific details & examples why *Goosebumps* are educational

#2   When kids start reading the *Goosebumps* books, as soon as they finish one book they want to buy another one or check one out of the library. Stine's stories are practically addicting! His plots cover a variety of subjects, so we learn as we read. *Goosebumps* stories get kids who don't normally like to read interested in reading.

One reason, specific details & examples why *Goosebumps* are scary

#3   If you're going to read your first *Goosebumps* story, let me give you a word of advice: don't read under the covers with a flashlight. It's too scary! Stine is known for creating the weirdest, scariest characters, like the bee boy in *Why I'm afraid Of Bees* and the counselor in *Camp Jelly Jam*. They give you the creeps! But, whether it's from a roller coaster, haunted house, or a terrifying book, kids like to be scared silly.

One reason, specific details & examples why *Goosebumps* are entertaining

#4   I get bored a lot. That's what's so good about having a new *Goosebumps* book. I can read anytime, and it makes the time pass faster. My mom complains about too much TV, so I read *Goosebumps* books instead. I always take one when I have to wait at the doctor's office or go on vacation with my parents.

Restate

Topic Sentence

Restate

3 Main Reasons

Conclusion

#5   When it comes to reading, you can't go wrong with a *Goosebumps* book. Not only do you learn some neat stuff, but they'll scare the daylights out of you. As long as you have a good book, you'll never get bored. Kids have to read a lot of things during the day, but the stories we like best of all are the scary, creepy *Goosebumps* books.

Name_____ Date_____

Would you enjoy going to a really cool theme park? Read about one below. Underline the main topic sentence. Circle each of the three main reasons.

THE NEATEST PLACE OF ALL!

Florida has beaches, pretty weather, and fun stuff to do. Each year thousands of tourists come to the sunshine state to visit Sea World, Disney World, Epcot, or Cypress Gardens. These parks are neat, but my personal favorite is Busch Gardens in Tampa. Live animals, awesome rides, and great shows are some of the reasons I like Busch Gardens.

For one thing, not too many other theme parks keep live animals. At Busch Gardens, you can visit the petting zoo. Kids can pet goats, chickens, and other small animals. They can feed them from their own hands. Other live animals are snakes, birds, apes, and an albino tiger. Busch Gardens is actually a zoo, with a nursery for newborn babies and a veterinary hospital. These buildings have glass walls so visitors can see what's going on.

After visiting the animals, you have to go on the Kumba! This roller coaster is one mile of twisted, nerve-wracking steel. Believe me, if you ever ride the Kumba, you'll never forget it. They strap you in carefully because you'll be turning completely upside down several times during your ride. If you survive the Kumba, there are several other good rides to choose from, like the Congo River Rapids and the Montu. My favorite is the log ride that ends in a humongous tidal wave. Woosh!

Before going home, you have to visit a few of the shows. Some are amazing, like the circus acts and high-wire trapeze artists. There's a funny show where people in the audience have to go up on stage, a bird show, and some musical shows. All these are good, but the one I like best is the ice-skating show. One man does some unbelievable juggling tricks while he's skating and he never misses.

Going to Busch Gardens is especially good because it has a little bit of everything. A great zoo, exciting rides, and entertaining shows are all at the same theme park. People may still go to all the big attractions in Orlando, but Busch Gardens in Tampa, Florida, is the one for me.

Name_____   Date_____

FIVE-PARAGRAPH-ESSAY PLANNER

Topic_____

Paragraph 1

Introduction _____

_____

Topic Sentence (Hook your reader!)

_____

_____

3 Main Reasons #1_____,

#2_____and #3_____.

Paragraph 2

Main Reason# 1 (Topic sentence for paragraph 2)

_____

_____

Specific Details or Examples _____,

_____, _____,

_____, _____.

Paragraph 3

Main Reason #2 (Topic sentence for paragraph 3)

_____

_____

Specific Details or Examples _____,

_____, _____,

_____, _____.

Paragraph 4

Main Reason #3 (Topic sentence for paragraph 4)

_____

_____

Specific Details or Examples _____,

_____, _____,

_____, _____.

Paragraph 5

Restate Topic Sentence _____

_____

Restate 3 Main Reasons #1_____,

#2_____, and #3_____.

Conclusion_____

_____

Reproducible exercise page

25 WAYS TO HELP PREPARE KIDS FOR WRITING-ASSESSMENT TESTS

1. Show many good examples. Let kids keep copies to analyze, mark, etc. Kids need to see what we expect from them.

2. Make sure your students are familiar with the word "prompt" and what it means. Show examples of many prompts. Discuss and brainstorm as a group, first. Then present a prompt for kids to brainstorm and organize on their own.

3. Teach writing "formulas" that help students stay organized. Look for organization in the good examples you have given students. Help kids see what an organizational plan looks like.

4. Show non-examples. Discuss how they differ from good examples.

5. Teach students to use a planning sheet. This should be on a paper that can be placed side by side with their paper (not on the back).

6. Teach students how to focus on a prompt. One technique is to write the prompt on sticky-notes and put them on their desks. Keep referring back to the prompt to make sure all writing stays focused directly on it.

7. Make sure titles are relatively short (3-5 words) They should be written last.

8. Allow kids to write in cursive or printing, whichever suits their creative style.

9. Show students how to sound out words they don't know how to spell. Show examples of "temporary" spelling. It's better for them to use a word that means exactly what they want to say, even if they can't spell it.

10. Discuss and show examples of precise word choices. Show students how to avoid using general or nonspecific words ("stuff," "things," "good,"etc.). Make a game of precise word-choice selection. Explain how one word may be adequate but another may be much better.

11. Model how revision and editing can be done between the lines, which leaves the rough draft neat and legible. Students may revise and edit their work on most writing-assessment tests. This is more important than just having a *neat* paper.

12. Show students specific ways to vary sentence structures. Practice doing this on the board. Praise their efforts!

13. Provide lists of transition words for students to memorize and keep in their Self-Contained Writer's Notebooks. Show how transition words tie thoughts together. Ask students to highlight transition words in their practice writing.

25 WAYS TO HELP PREPARE...

14. Stress writing an introduction, middle, and conclusion. The conclusion is usually the weakest area of writing. Teach kids to go back and check the conclusion after they think they've finished.

15. Teach students how to support their explanations and arguments with many specific details and examples. Put examples and non-examples on the board. Show students how to write all important reasons first.

16. Teach the basic conventions of spelling, punctuation, and capitalization. Train students to become student editors, able to correct peer writing as well as their own. It is difficult for any writer to see personal mistakes. Knowing everyone makes mistakes is the first step toward objectivity.

17. Have students write a number at the top of their papers instead of their names when practicing writing. This helps with objectivity when looking for errors on peer papers.

18. Practice timing kids for the same amount of time they'll have on the test. Be sure to notify kids when they have 10 minutes left. Praise writers who budget time to plan, write, and, most of all, *revise!*

19. Help students collect lists of *degree words*, such as big, large, giant, huge, humongous, gigantic, gargantuan, etc. to be used in description.

20. Read good descriptive passages from literature aloud often. This stimulates kids' ability to describe. Selections may be short. Encourage students to find such passages on their own and share with the class.

21. Make transparencies of student writing and discuss them as a class. Encourage students to point out ways the writer could improve a piece. Be sure to call attention to things the writer did that added to the piece.

22. Familiarize your students with the rubric that will be used on their writing-assessment test. Discuss the scoring and the qualities the scorers are looking for. Show examples of papers that have been scored.

23. Ask another teacher or educator to score a set of practice papers according to the same rubric that will be used on the test. Let kids review their scores and make improvements.

24. Invite parents to come in for an evening of writing. Familiarize them with the skills and formulas students need for good expository writing. Enlist their help to work *with* you, at home, by showing interest in their child's writing.

25. Make the writing-test day a positive experience. Plan a post-test party, buy T-shirts, ring bells, or have an outside picnic. Celebrate! Writing accomplishments need as much hoopla as sporting events. Invite volunteers, principals, and parents to share your students' success.

Expository Writing Practice Prompts

While I clearly favor letting kids choose their writing topics as often as possible, it is still important for them to be able to write to a given prompt. Here are a few examples of prompts worded in the style you might see on a writing-assessment test. Notice the importance of thinking & prewriting.

Our state is an interesting place to live.
 A. Before writing, think about reasons why our state is interesting.
 B. List your reasons.
 C. Now explain why these reasons make Florida interesting.

Families are important.
 A. Before you write, think about why your family is important.
 B. Make a list of these reasons.
 C. Now explain why your family is important to you.

When we practice doing something we get better at it.
 A. Think of something you like to do that requires some practice.
 B. List the different ways you practice.
 C. Now explain why practice helps you improve.

Everyone has a favorite teacher.
 A. Before you begin writing, think about your favorite teacher.
 B. List a few examples that make this teacher your favorite.
 C. Now explain why this teacher is your favorite.

Someday you will select a career (job).
 A. Think of a career you would enjoy.
 B. List some of the specific reasons you would like this career.
 C. Now explain why you would like this career.

We can get exercise in many different ways.
 A. Think of a form of exercise you enjoy.
 B. Before you start writing, think of a few reasons you like this form of exercise.
 C. Now explain why this exercise is fun and good for you.

Some people think kids shouldn't watch television on school nights.
 A. Decide if you agree or disagree with that view.
 B. List reasons to support your opinion.
 C. Now try to convince your reader to believe the way you do by supporting your opinion with reasons and examples.

It takes the right kind of person to be a responsible pet owner.
 A. Think of qualities that make a good pet owner.
 B. List several important reasons to support your thoughts.
 C. Now describe the qualities that would make a responsible pet owner and give examples.

ASSESSMENT

How Do You Put A "Pricetag" On Expression?

Since I'm a writer myself, I always feel a bit of empathy when it comes down to assessing and evaluating another's written thoughts and creativity. The subjectivity of writing requires our involvement not only as teachers but as coauthors in order to fully assess the understanding and *accomplishment of writing*. There is no answer key. The entire process has to be taken into consideration. The whole kit and caboodle.

Yet, as teachers, we want to know our students are progressing as writers. We want to know our methods and strategies are propelling them towards independent thinking and expressive creativity. We must evaluate whether we are meeting the individual needs of our students. But how?

To Grade, Or Not To Grade? That Is The Question.

For centuries teachers have lugged home huge stacks of writing papers to grade while the rest of their family watch hilarious television programs and eat popcorn. The plight was especially arduous for English teachers, for they were constantly assailed by compositions, themes, research papers, and short stories. These poor souls, identified by permanent writer's cramp and red ink stains on their clothing, became bitter recluses, mere shells of their former selves, and had to be locked up in towers or hospitals for the hopeless. For them, there was no light at the end of the tunnel.

Students anticipated the return of their papers almost as much as getting a root canal. The teacher's pet had her paper handed back first, grade side up so the entire class could gaze with rapt envy at the A+ neatly emblazoned in the upper corner. The other papers, resembling road maps, were discretely turned grade side down and handed back with a scowl. Mine usually had "See me during recess today!" scrawled where I would have liked to have seen a smiley face. For us it was either conform or clap erasers. I clapped.

Only 9,876 to go...

I know teachers who actually have driven to other towns to secretly throw away old stacks of writing assignments they never had time to grade. Others live with the specter of guilt hanging over them because they are three months behind. A few teachers I know hedge about teaching writing because they don't want to have to grade. Stop grading! Get a life!

Instead, start assessing student writing. There's a huge difference. Grading attempts to put an objective grade on a subjective discipline. Assessing takes the whole picture into consideration: progress, creativity, skills mastered, content. *The American Heritage Dictionary* defines "assessment" as to evaluate, *appraise*. Your focus will be on students as authors, not as conformists to one set of standards. Our goals should be to know our children as authors, evaluate their progress, and meet their individual needs.

The difference between grading and assessing is radical. Imagine. I give you $20,000 to design your "dream room" at home. It can be anything you want it to be: wood-working shop, gourmet kitchen, or couch potato paradise. You have two months to design and create. If I grade you, I tell you how I think you should design the room, wait until you have completed the project and then judge your efforts. "This is out of place," I say. "This would have been better over there. I like your choice of carpet, but why didn't you select another color for the walls?"

On the other hand, if I am assessing you, it is important to me to know what style of room you choose and why. I am available for counsel all during the building process. I drop by every day to check on your progress. "What a good idea!" I enthuse. "You might want to consider making the door a bit wider if you want to get the piano through, though." Every now and then I sit down with you to study the plans, to guide, and to evaluate your progress. Together we celebrate your accomplishments.

I realize parents and administrators expect us to grade. There are ways to grade students on the mastery of certain skills, but these need to be tested objectively. It is acceptable to give a writing-workshop grade based on participation, time on task, cooperation, organization, etc. It is also acceptable to test kids on certain aspects of the writing process, but they need to be told ahead of time exactly what you are looking for.

However, I am not for "grading" writing pieces that stem from the joyous overflow of a child's thoughts, emotions, or creativity. The ultimate reward for an author is not a grade, but to be read and appreciated by readers.

Time Alone With The Teacher!

Nothing takes the place of one-on-one time between teacher and student. There is no substitute when it comes to personal attention. Yet there are so many of "them" and only one of you. How do you do it?

Make a personal appointment with each student once a month. If your class size is smaller, you can meet more often. Give out appointment cards. Display a large appointment calendar with each time slot and student's name. Schedule appointments throughout the month—not all during one week. I usually recommend starting out with 15-30 minute appointments, then tailoring the time to suit your needs.

MONTH

DON'T FORGET THE DATE! 25

Ask kids in advance to be prepared for your time together. They will bring their Self-Contained Writer's Notebook and several pieces or writing projects they have been working on. They need to present a final form or at least a rough draft that has passed through a student editor first. This will save valuable time so you don't have to look for picky things such as question marks and capital letters. You will look for good writing content, structure, strengths, revision, creativity, etc.

I like to look carefully at one or two pieces, give help, compliments, suggestions, talk with the writer about revisions, and ask the writer if and how the piece will be published. Since I've been circulating during the daily writing workshop, I'm already familiar with what my students are working on and have conferred on a daily basis. The writing appointment is an intensive time of one-on-one attention, evaluation, affirmation, and accountability. I notice and comment on how much progress has been made. We discuss strengths and weaknesses. We discuss goals to work on and new things to try. We make decisions together about putting pieces in the student's writing portfolio. If time allows, I also flip through the Self-Contained Writer's Notebook to see how other projects are coming. I make sure students know that I am available

Terrific!

It was a dark and stormy night...

before school, during writing workshops, and at other times to read and celebrate their writing all during the month. Most of all, I validate all positive progress the student has made as an *author.*

Student Responsibility!

About one week before your writing appointment you might remind, "Andrea, we have an appointment together next Thursday, and I'm so looking forward to seeing some of the things you've been working on. Will you please get some pieces ready to share with me? If you'll see a student editor and will make corrections before our appointment, we'll have more time to discuss your writing. If you're having any problems, I'll be glad to help you with them then." It is now the student's responsibility to select pieces, meet with a student editor, make changes, and prepare for the appointment. Part of your writing grade, if you have to give one, can be based on preparation for the appointment, organization, and personal accomplishment.

Don't worry about students recopying a piece if the rough draft is legible. Together you are going to make changes and revisions, anyway, so that step is wasted energy. It is very freeing for students to know they don't have to copy over until they are ready to publish. I still am shocked to find teachers who rank neatness as the number one criteria for good writing. After your appointment, after all corrections, revisions, editing and proofreading have been done, and if the student is going to publish the piece in some way, then is the time to recopy, type on the computer, put in book form, frame, hang up, present, record, perform, or read to the class.

Classroom Management

Ah, you say. Sounds good on paper, but how do you pull it off with 25 other little critters all demanding your attention? Training, my dears, training. Your class should understand that during writing appointments you will devote yourself to one student unless there is an absolute emergency.  Post a sign or flag reading: ***Private appointment in session. Do not disturb!*** Another strategy is to train a classroom greeter, equipped with pencil and notepad, to politely

NOTES:

greet guests who come to the door when I am in an appointment with the message, "I'm sorry, but Mrs. Forney is having a private appointment with a writer. May I take a message for you?" (When I tell workshop audiences this, they always howl.) Of course, let your principal and other teachers know your strategy beforehand. You don't want to appear rude. The purpose is to let children feel their time alone with you is valuable and is to be guarded. How many times do we cut them off—even mid-sentence—to greet an "important" visitor at the door. Writing appointments are times I want children to have my undivided attention.

- **Make appointments early**
- **Give appointment cards**
- **Post on class calendar**
- **Remind kids in advance**
- **Positive reinforcement**
- **One-on-one time**

WRITING APPOINTMENT

Name_____

Date_____

Time_____

THANK YOU FOR VISITING...

Dear Visitor,

Since I am in a highly important meeting with one of my student authors, I cannot be disturbed unless it is an emergency.

I will be available to meet with you in a few minutes if you'd like to wait, or you can leave a written message.

Sincerely,

MESSAGE: _____

_____

_____

_____

The Writing Appointment

The stage is set. Your students are busy at work in writing workshop, and it is time for your appointment with Andrea. You invite her to join you at a table for two over to one side of the classroom. You raise the *Do Not Disturb* flag or whatever signal you've prearranged with your class, and your classroom greeter will keep an eye on the door. If you're one of the lucky teachers who has an assistant or volunteer, this is an ideal time to have him circulate in the workshop.

Your goal, for the next 15-30 minutes, is to find out more about Andrea as a writer, to read and respond to her work, discuss new writing goals, and to teach her individually.

Teacher: (She reads Andrea's fairy tale narrative.) This has really turned out to be a nice story. I'm impressed!

Andrea: I've been working on it all week.

Teacher: I love the ending. How did you think of that?

Andrea: I just changed it yesterday. I worked on it some last night.

Teacher: I laughed out loud! You've got to share that with the class.

Andrea: Okay.

Teacher: How do you feel about the piece?

Andrea: Pretty good...there are a few rough spots, I guess.

Teacher: Is there anything you'd like me to help you with?

Andrea: Yeah, the dialogue...right...here. See? (She reads a bit.) It doesn't sound right.

Teacher: I know what you mean. I had trouble knowing who was talking at that point. Do you think the queen would say, "Who is in the tower?"

Andrea: What do you mean?

Teacher: Well, your dialogue was so witty up to that point. Then the queen's response is confusing. Can you work on that?

Andrea: You mean, have her say something like she did to the knight? About her royal privileges?

Teacher: Exactly. Good idea. Just work on it. I like the way you've got dialogue all through the piece. The kids are going to go wild over that. (Teacher reads further.) Look at this...you've got the word "great" in this sentence, and here it is again, right in the next sentence. What could you substitute there?

Andrea: Hmm...good?

Teacher: Too ordinary. We use that word for so many things. Think.

NOTES:

Andrea:	Fantastic?
Teacher:	Better. (She smiles.)
Andrea:	Extraordinary? Tremendous? (She smiles.)
Teacher:	Now you're cookin'. Substitute one of those. Well, Andrea, you've worked hard on this, and it really shows. I see lots of progress in your writing. What do you think?
Andrea:	I love writing dialogue like you showed us. I didn't know how.
Teacher:	You see how it makes your characters come alive. I think you've got the hang of it. I sure could use you to teach that concept in a small group. Several kids still are having some trouble with dialogue.
Andrea:	What helped me the most was when you recorded our conversation and then had us write it down.
Teacher:	Well, your story is a winner. What do you plan to do with it?
Andrea:	I thought about making it into a book.
Teacher:	That's an idea. I think you're going to have quite a few readers if you do. Do you want to use the computer or do it by hand?
Andrea:	I want to draw the pictures myself and make one of those books like Mrs. Forrester helped us with.
Teacher:	That'll work well. Let me know if you need any help. Did you finish the poem about your grandmother?
Andrea:	Almost. I can't think of an ending. (She reads poem aloud.) See? I get to that point and get stuck.
Teacher:	How did you feel when your grandmother helped you plant the rosebush?
Andrea:	Sad. (Pause) I knew she wouldn't live long enough to see the roses grow. But I was glad because we did it together.
Teacher:	Could you tell us that? It's okay to let your reader know how you felt. Everyone has known some kind of loss, so they should be able to relate to the tone of your poem.
Andrea:	I'll try. I really want to finish it. I'd like to frame it for my mom.
Teacher:	I'm sure that would be a special gift. And it's good to let your mom know how much her mother meant to you. (Pause) Is there something you'd like me to teach you?
Andrea:	(She thinks.) Well...I'd like to write a play next time. I don't know how to get started with all the directions and stuff.
Teacher:	I'd be happy to show you how. When you think of what your play is going to be about and have a plan, I'll show you how to write the staging directions. Just let me know any day in writing workshop, and we can work on it together.

Ask the Author!

Part of our job as authors is to try to put what we think into words. Authors love to answer questions about their writing and about what goes on in their heads. As teachers, we can find some of our most valuable insights about children by asking questions and listening. If you want to assess a writer's work and writing progress, ask questions.

How are you doing as an author? What are your strengths? Weaknesses? How are you improving? What are some things you're learning as a writer? How did you learn those things? How have you changed since the beginning of the year? What are some pieces you'd like to write? Which is your favorite piece of the ones you've been working on? Why? How can I help you? Is there anything you'd like me to teach you? Is there a specific subject you're interested in?

Take notes. Record your findings. Keep some sort of record system on each child. Know your writers. Knowing them is the key to reaching them. Validate their fears, insecurities, successes, and accomplishments.

Younger children sometimes need a teacher's encouragement to expand writing beyond a few sentences until they get the hang of it. Writing-appointment discussions have a way of showing kids how much information they already know and commissioning them to write.

Teacher:	I'm glad to see that you've been busy writing, Tameeka. Will you read your story? I'd like to hear it.
Tameeka:	"Last Saturday I went to the beach with my mama and aunt. We had fun. I like the beach. Do you like the beach?"
Teacher:	What a nice beginning. I love stories about the beach. Where's the rest of your story? I want to hear more.
Tameeka:	I can't think of any more.
Teacher:	(Smiles) The kids in our classroom are going to want to know all about what happened at the beach. Could you give us some more details? I like the way you described your camping trip. Remember?
Tameeka:	I guess so. But I can't think of anything else.
Teacher:	Did you guys buy hot dogs for lunch at the beach?
Tameeka:	No. My mama made a picnic.
Teacher:	What fun. What all did she pack?
Tameeka:	We had fried chicken, potato salad, pickles, cake—it

99

NOTES:

	was chocolate cake—and eggs. The hard kind you have to peel.
Teacher:	Be sure to include that in your story. Writers need to make their readers taste, smell, see, imagine... Okay now...We need some action in your story. I bet a day at the beach was more fun than being at school, right? (Laughs) What are some of the things you did that kids like to do at the beach?
Tameeka:	We swam. And we rode floats. I have a new float shaped like a dolphin. My daddy bought it for me.
Teacher:	Now you're thinking like a writer. That's the good stuff we like to hear about—details.
Tameeka:	I rode on the waves with my new float, and my daddy dug up some sand dollars with his toes. Oh—I forgot—we made sand castles.
Teacher:	Sand castles? My children and I like to do that, too, but I always get so sunburned. Did anyone help you, or did you do it by yourself?
Tameeka:	My sister. We made a big, old sand castle, and then the waves came and knocked it down. Ruined it.
Teacher:	I have an idea! Why don't you go back and add some to your story? You could tell us about the picnic, and swimming, and the sand castle. I know the kids are really going to want to hear all about it when it's your turn to share in the Author's Chair.
Tameeka :	You think so? I could tell about the sand dollars, too.
Teacher:	Are you the same girl who told me you couldn't think of anything else to say? (Smiles) You're doing a great job with words. Before you forget all this good stuff, would you take a few minutes to add it to your story? I'll come back in a few minutes and see if you need any help remembering.

Writing Appointment Questions

Besides evaluating student writing progress, the writing-appointment is also time to help young authors grow as writers. Give careful attention to reading their pieces. Besides discussing the subject or topic, utilize this opportunity to discuss how the author arrived at writing the text.

Select a few key questions to ask the author about his piece. Questioning helps us think about aspects of writing we may have overlooked. It helps us grow as authors to look for evidence in our writing.

WRITING-DISCUSSION QUESTIONS

Does the first sentence grab the reader's attention?

Does the first paragraph introduce the reader to the subject?

Would the reader know where and when the story takes place?

Do we know enough details about the main characters?

Is the conflict interesting or exciting?

Do the characters seem real?

Does the dialogue sound the way people talk?

Will readers know who is doing the talking?

Do transition words help the paragraphs flow together?

Does the narrative stay in first or third person?

Is there enough action to keep the reader interested till the end?

Is there a sentence that doesn't quite make sense?

Is there a particular word readers might not know?

Are there any passive verbs you could change to active verbs?

Did you use specific words to describe sounds, tastes, textures, etc.?

Could you combine any sentences and still have the same meaning?

Is there any part that's boring or dull?

Are there several exciting (humorous, scary, etc.) parts?

Does the story shine with something fresh and new?

Could this possibly be seen as a rip-off of another story?

Does the title reveal too much?

Does the solution resolve the conflict?

Does the conclusion let the reader down gently?

Is the story suited to the age of your audience?

Have you used a variety of sentence beginnings?

Does the narrative or dialogue repeat itself too much?

Is the story organized with a beginning, middle, and ending?

Are there any unanswered questions the reader might have?

Would a plot device add to the story? (Flashback, twist, surprise)

Have you written anything that wouldn't be appropriate for kids?

Record Keeping

In order to be the best teachers we possibly can be, we have to know what our students know about writing. Each child's strengths and weaknesses, successes and failures help shape our teaching strategies and goals. Because children are important, record keeping is important.

Keep some sort of system to track and record your students' progress. Take notes during writing workshops and writing appointments. Save samples and examples that illustrate individual needs. Use these notes to develop child-centered curriculum and to target kids who need help or remediation. If you are required to give a writing grade, keep records and examples of how and why you arrived at your findings.

Each student's Self-Contained Writer's Notebook will have dozens of examples of works in progress, peer editing sheets, critiques, writing topic ideas, revisions, etc. The notebook itself is a valuable record to show parents and principals the process of writing as well as ongoing works. Whenever I show parents a particular writing piece, I like to have a record of every step a child has completed: prewriting, rough draft complete with revisions, response and editing sheets, and publication.

Writing Portfolios

One of my earliest memories of writing is that it was expendable. We wrote during the week, and on Friday the papers were stapled together to "go home," a traditional ritual. A few were emblazoned on our refrigerator or put in a scrapbook, but the bulk just disappeared in the same burial ground where elephants go to die.

A writing portfolio is a growing collection of student work samples in all stages. It is a record-keeping system of how a writer has progressed in different genres, skills, and interests. Stipulating a list of genres that must go in it only turns the portfolio into a standardized requirement. Instead, collaborate with each student to decide which pieces have something important to show or say. A writing portfolio is a time capsule of sorts that depicts a student's interests, tastes, capabilities, and accomplishments. While it can be used for documentation, remember that a portfolio is also a highly personal collection *owned by the writer.*

STUDENT WRITING PORTFOLIOS

The Definition

As the name suggests, this collection is a wide range of writing samples produced by a single student throughout the year or years.

The Purpose

A portfolio provides an ongoing bank of writing examples for enjoyment, assessment, and personal growth.

"Through writing children build a sense of who they are and become sensitive to the views of others."
Dr. Linda Lamme, *Growing Up Writing*

Skills Reinforced by Student Writing Portfolio

- expository writing
- narrative writing
- critical thinking
- evaluating
- editing
- revising

- sequencing
- research
- organization
- neatness
- collecting
- time management

Possible Contents

The decision of what pieces to put in the portfolio should be a collaboration between teacher and student writer.

Table of Contents
Photo of Author
Favorite Piece
Best Piece
Teacher's Choice
Early Writing
Examples of Improvement
Favorite Genres
Strengths
Weaknesses
Rough Drafts
Revisions
Personal Selections
Published Works

Make sure to date all selections

The Value

A student writing portfolio is an excellent way to foster good writing skills and enable students to collect a showcase of their various writing experiences and genres. By stressing the importance of saving and savoring expressive writing, teachers encourage students to collect samples of peer editing, response, revision, editing, and publishing. The writing portfolio becomes a personal writing history.

The repertoire of samples can be used as a record of writing improvement, documenting progress for teachers and parents.

PUBLISHING

Celebrate Accomplishment!

I'll never forget the day my first children's book arrived from the publisher. I saw the postal worker arrive, lugging a heavy box towards my front door. He never made it. I met him halfway and practically wrestled the box from him. With trembling fingers, I tore into the box and there, on the cover of the new books, was *my name*. It was living proof that I was really an author. Children soon would be able to check out my book from the library! My first impulse was to tell someone—anyone—who could help me celebrate. My next impulse was to start another book, and I did.

Those same reactions can belong to the authors in your room. Kids have the same desire to have their work read, appreciated, and celebrated as any other writer. Writing is a lot of hard work, especially after you've gone through all steps of the writing process. To realize a final product is a heady experience, one that drives most authors back to the creative drawing board. Publishing begats more writing, new risks, fresh goals, expanded vision.

Publishing Formats

When teachers talk about publishing, they tend to think in terms of handmade or spiral bound picture books written by each child. That is an important format of publishing, but not by any means the only format. As discussed in Chapter 9, the writing workshop tries to provide opportunities for "real" writing that is used for valid purposes. Mailing a letter is a form of publishing. So is producing a play, presenting a puppet show, contributing to a school newspaper, singing a song written by a young lyricist, having an editorial accepted for publication in a city newspaper, or producing a giant poster about the life cycle of a butterfly.

Debbie Brady publishes an annual classroom anthology of student writing that is an anticipated keepsake. Karen Paul publishes a monthly classroom newspaper with an assortment of student articles.

One of my most successful "publications" was an elegant evening soirée complete with fancy dresses for the girls and ties for the boys. We invited parents, studied etiquette, made delicious hors d'oeuvres, and entertained our guests with an hour of poetry, vignettes, essays, and music. Look for creative ways to publish a variety of genres produces by your students. Not only is this good for the author, but gives other writers ideas and provides cultural experiences for your entire class.

Magazines For Kids

Did you know there are more than 300 magazines just for kids, and many of them—most of them—publish poetry, riddles, illustrations, jokes, short stories, photos, and expository pieces written by children. *Cricket, Humpty Dumpty, Child Life, Children's Digest, Stone Soup, Ranger Rick, Sports Illustrated For Kids, Owl Magazine, Calliope, Jack and Jill, Highlights For Children, U*S* Kids, Clubhouse Jr., and National Geographic World,* are just a few. Your school media center and public library contain other sources. Many of these periodicals are more than happy to send you one complimentary copy for classroom use. Check inside information for editor's name, title, and address. Be sure to submit children's writing, illustrations, or photos early, as magazines tend to plan issues months ahead of time.

In-House Publishing Company

We all know teachers are incredibly busy just trying to teach the writing process to a roomful of children. To add the publishing process to those responsibilities is almost too much for any teacher when you consider the amount of writing that will be going on in your classroom.

Enlist the help of your PTA, PTO, interested parents, friends, and volunteers to help form an in-house publishing company for your entire school. This will benefit every child and teacher, as classes can order blank books or send writing pieces to be bound. Set up the company in a central location and establish an assembly line system.

Be It Henceforth Known That On

The _____ Day of _____, 199__

The _____ Elementary School Publishing Company

Was Formed at

_____

Principal

Media Specialist

Writing Consultant

Participants

Materials For Publishing

Ask your in-house publishing company to gather plenty of materials so children may publish all year long. As with classroom writing supplies, these materials can be donated from different sources in the community.

If your school has publishing machines, such as spiral binders, this can speed up the process. If not, handmade books are fine. As a matter of fact, once older children have been shown how to make handmade books they can continue to "publish" at home, saving classroom time for actual writing. Some media specialists will provide library envelopes for the books so they can be checked out of the media center or classroom.

Instructions For Publishing Handmade Books

1. Cut cardboard covers
   8 & 1/2" X 5 & 1/2" (vertical or horizontal)
   8 & 1/2" X 11"

2. Cover with:
   plain paper, colored paper, wall paper, maps, magazine pictures, fabric
   Cut cover 1/2" larger than cardboard
   Snip corners, fold in and glue to cardboard using rubber cement

3. Make insides of book
   5-20 white pages, cut 1/2" smaller than cardboard cover
   add flyleaf to front, face down, back pages to back, face up
   Staple together, 3 staples, close to edge

4. Put insides between cardboard covers with
   stapled edge sticking out 1/3"

5. Cut duct tape or library tape a little longer than cardboard

6. Lay covers and insides on duct tape

7. Cut off tape even with covers

8. Glue down fly leaf to inside cover, back page to back cover

9. Fold back to form hinge

10. Fill orders for teachers and students

(Glue this page to inside back cover)

ABOUT THE AUTHOR

_____

_____

_____

_____

_____

(Make this the last stapled page of book)

I READ YOUR BOOK

SIGNATURE	THE PART I LIKE BEST IS...

(Glue flyleaf to inside front cover)

WRITTEN BY

_____

PUBLISHED BY

_____ ELEMENTARY SCHOOL

_____

199___

WRITTEN BY

_____

PUBLISHED BY

_____ ELEMENTARY SCHOOL

_____

199___

(Glue flyleaf to inside front cover)

Puppet Stage

Young authors love to write puppet plays, make the characters, and produce original plays for their peers. This form of "publishing" provides not only the appreciation and validation an author needs, but an enjoyable experience for your other students.

I particularly like puppet plays because they entail not only writing a play, but making sure the plot is revealed through dialogue. Then the author must choose classmates to manipulate the puppets, practice, and present the play to a live audience. Talk about a collaboration! If you have several budding playwrights, you can have several productions going at once. If the plays turn out well, invite other classes to join in the audience, perhaps starting a cultural exchange right in your school.

You can buy puppet stages through educational catalogues, but the best ones I've found are those made from PVC pipe, two by fours, and simple hardware. A puppet stage is easy to make, inexpensive, and portable. It can be stored out of the way in a trunk when not in use. Again, don't get involved in making the stage yourself. Instead, enlist the help of a talented parent or community carpenter. Ask someone you know who sews to make a curtain from black remnant material found at discount stores.

Classroom Podium

According to a recent poll, most people's number one fear is having to speak in public. If we start kids while they're young, in the accepting, nurturing environment of their classrooms, we can help them develop a positive attitude towards public speaking, an asset they could use their entire lives.

When "publishing" original speeches, make sure kids have a lectern from which to speak, a place for their notes, and a live microphone, if possible. Practice presenting speeches in front of a video camera so speakers can review and see areas that need improvement. Public speaking is a persuasive form of "publishing" for the author as well as the audience because a writer is presenting his work orally, and the inflection and emphasis in his voice are powerful tools of communication.

Publishing Software

Computer software and the Internet have drastically changed the face of communication and publishing. To deprive kids of these rich experiences is to cheat them out of knowledge and a competitive edge with others who are computer literate.

Take advantage of on-line writing help and publishing opportunities such as America Online's Kids Only Menu or *CyberKids*, an online magazine for kids that can be reached at http://www.mtlake.com/cyberkids. Both provide exciting opportunities for kids to "publish" their writing online and for other kids to read it and respond. Your students will be able to publish their writing pieces for a worldwide audience!

New publishing software programs are coming out every day, so check the catalogues, contact software companies on the Internet, or visit preview centers near you.

Software	Company	Level
Imagination Express Series CD	Edmark	Grades K-6
Electro Dog's First Reader/Writer CD	Orange Cherry	Grades K-4
Talking First Writer	Orange Cherry	Grades 1-4
Young Authors	Underdog Educational	Grades 1 +
Writing About Children's Literature	Heartsoft	Grades 3-8
Writer's Workshops-Learning to Write	Heartsoft	Grades 4-12
Storybook Maker Deluxe CD	Hartley	Grades K-3
My Words	Hartley	Grades K-4
Make-A-Book	Teacher Support	Grades K-4
Write Now	Softkey	Grades 4 +
Big Book Maker Series	Toucan	Grades 1 +
The Amazing Writing Machine	Broderbund	Grades K-8
Creative Writer	Microsoft	Grades 3 +
Bank Street Writer	Scholastic	Grades 3-12
Process Writer	Scholastic	Grades 4-7
Write On!	Humanities	Grades K-6
Hollywood CD	Theatrix	Grades 4 +
Storybook Weaver Deluxe CD	MECC	Grades 1-6
The Children's Writing & Publishing Center	The Learning Company	Grades 2-9
Student Writing Center	The Learning Company	Grades 4 +
What's My Story?	Broderbund	Grades 2-6
Opening Night	MECC	Grades 3-6

YOUNG AUTHORS' CONFERENCE

Recognizing Achievement

Working with Mr. Joachim was a writing consultant's dream. From day-one I knew there was something different about this elementary school principal. He didn't just spout rhetoric: kids came first at his school, and everything else was planned around that philosophy. Any writing idea could come to fruition, any project, realized. You could almost never find him in his office but you could almost always find him in the hallway talking to kids or sitting in their classrooms taking notice of what they were writing. When it came time to plan the Young Authors' Conference, Mr. Joachim completely immersed himself in every step of planning, making sure his young writers' efforts would be rewarded appropriately. Every school should be so lucky.

We live in a day and age where sports are recognized in global olympics, beauty pageant contestants compete worldwide, and movie stars are elevated to "superhero" status. Yet at the same time, some of the worthiest accomplishments are going on right under our noses. When students progress from fledgling writers to published authors, we need to recognize their achievement. The Young Authors' Conference is the perfect way to end your year, and something every school should consider, since it recognizes and validates children who have become authors and published a body of work.

What Is A Young Authors' Conference?

A Young Authors' Conference is a day, or several days, set aside to highlight student writing accomplishments. It can entail mini-workshops to foster new writing ideas, student displays throughout the school, special guests, and an assembly program where selected works will be read or presented, awards given, and authors recognized. You might want to start small and "grow" each year.

Planning: Get Everyone Involved!

Your Young Authors' Conference can be one of the biggest events of the school calendar, one that students, teachers, parents, and guests look forward to each year. In order to be successful, however, you'll need the complete support of your principal, every teacher, and of course, kids.

Start Early

Start planning the Young Authors' Conference early in the year. If teachers don't feel they have to rush or push kids to complete writing projects, they'll have a much better outlook. There will be time to order awards, to form various committees, and to plan teaching with the conference in mind.

Divide and Conquer: Form Committees

Invite teachers, student representatives, administrators, and parents to serve on planning committees. Schedule individual meetings throughout the year and keep your faculty posted on the progress. Hype the writing conference all year, heightening the excitement as the day draws near.

Individual Committees

GUEST AUTHOR

A special draw for a Young Authors' Conference is inviting a children's author to your school. Kids love meeting a real, live author, and if you get one who is a good speaker or will hold some mini-workshops for kids, so much the better. You can book authors through their publishers, agents, local librarians, and writers' groups. A check of your area might yield a stable of children's authors from which to choose.

Call or invite the children's author early in the year to match your conference to his schedule. Provide all pertinent information and ask about fees. Most guest authors charge a speaking fee, ranging from $50 - $1,000 plus traveling expenses. Make arrangements to have the author's books on sale during the conference and let children and parents know the titles and prices in advance. Check back with the author a time or two during the year to verify all arrangements. Make hotel reservations, if necessary, and provide a guide to stay with the author throughout the visit. Furnishing bottled water, fresh flowers, or a "goodie" basket for your visiting author are extra touches that say, "Welcome!"

WRITING MINI-WORKSHOPS

Writing workshops are an option that encourage and create a feeling of camaraderie for your young writers. Plan several mini-workshops or clinics students can sign up for and attend during the Young Authors' Conference. Presenters can be older students, visiting high school students, teachers, local celebrities, community college professors, etc. Workshops could include such subjects as *Illustrating, Writing on the Internet, How To Make Your Characters Come Alive With Dialogue,* etc. A workshop for parents and guests is one way to make them feel included.

CERTIFICATES, RIBBONS, BUTTONS, AND TROPHIES

A memorable experience like a Young Authors' Conference should be marked by keepsake mementos kids can proudly display in their bedrooms along with 4-H ribbons and sports trophies. Make sure to print enough so every child who has published something during the year can receive one. I like the idea of presenting kids with a ribbon or button they can wear throughout the conference and a trophy or certificate they can cherish. These are available through educational catalogues, specialty stores, or imprinting companies. If your budget would not allow the purchase of these, see if a corporate sponsor will underwrite or donate the cost. Tangible "awards" make the day special.

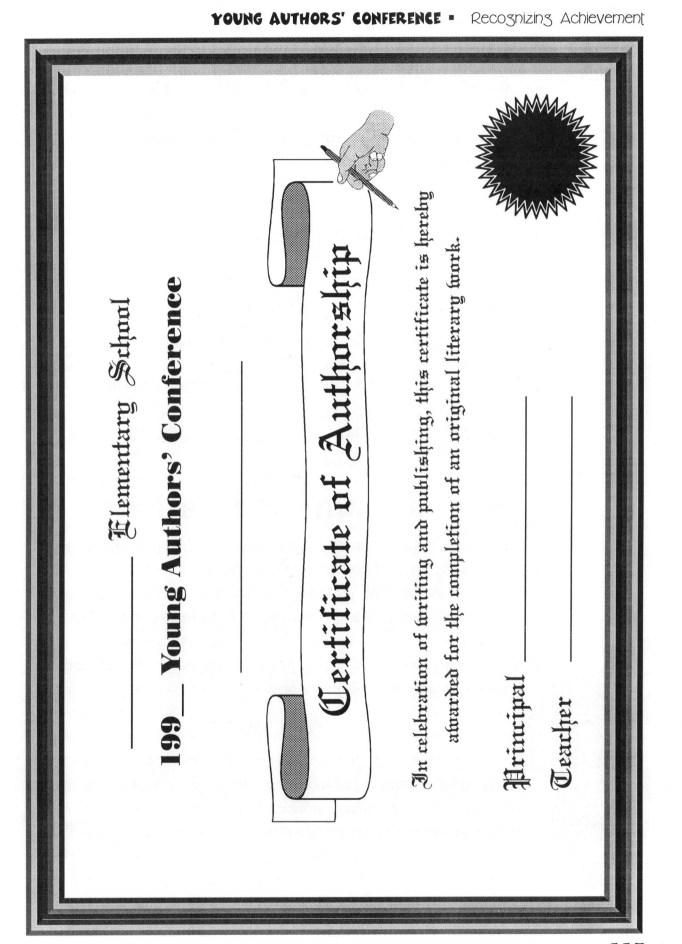

Elementary School

199__ Young Authors' Conference

Certificate of Authorship

In celebration of writing and publishing, this certificate is hereby awarded for the completion of an original literary work.

Principal

Teacher

NOTES:

INVITATIONS & PRINTED PROGRAMS

Children can be involved in designing, addressing, and delivering invitations to parents and guests. This committee will design and print a program of the Young Authors' Conference events, including names of presenters, guest author, and young authors who will present their work.

PUBLICITY & MEDIA

Create a media frenzy at your school. Pull out all the stops! Put up posters, publicize in the newspaper, take photos, tape "spots" for morning announcements, interview young authors, get your administrators to participate in zany skits or contests which generate anticipation of the conference. The sky is the limit! Plan a countdown, bury a time capsule, have a hot air balloon land on the playground, sound horns, ring buzzers, anything to help you blitz this event! Ask a local reporter or a parent who's into photography to take photos on the day of the conference. Make sure to get photos of your kids posing with the visiting author.

DECORATIONS & THEME

It's always fun to have a theme around which you can center the decorations, colors, and mementos of the Young Authors' Conference. It can be as simple as "Writing Makes The World Go Round" or as complex as a "Writing Rodeo," "Writing Olympics," "Grand Prix of Writing," etc. At any rate, go all out! The conferences I've been involved with as a guest author or writing consultant have knocked my socks off with charming decorations and were affairs kids would remember the rest of their lives.

MUSIC

Music is one of those simple little touches that adds so much to a conference for children. A pre-taped cassette comes in handy and can be used to provide a musical background for kids while they are entering and exiting the auditorium. Grandiose music can be played to recognize your authors when they enter; a live band playing in the hall or foyer can greet your guests as they arrive. Your choral music teacher might work up a musical contribution.

STUDENT DISPLAYS

All writing deserves to be read, enacted, sung, or presented. Of course, that would be impossible in a school setting, so displays are a way to showcase writing 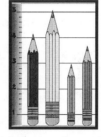 throughout the classrooms, halls, media center, offices, and cafeteria. Each teacher can be responsible for displaying students' writing as creatively as possible. Writing samples from different genres can be collected all throughout the year for display. While most pices will be in final published form, a few pieces might be used to show the steps writers must go through to revise and improve their writing.

SCHEDULE OF EVENTS

Someone has to keep things moving along and to plan times and locations for the conference. Be sure to include an administrator on this committee so you can coordinate schedule changes that might effect your cafeteria staff and janitors. Post the schedule several weeks before the conference so teachers will know how to plan.

USHERS & TOUR GUIDES

Reliable, older students make great ushers to give out printed programs, greet and direct visitors at the front door of the school, and give tours of student work throughout the school. Official badges or arm bands make ushers and tour guides easy to identify. Their assistance will make your conference run smoothly. Students will have an opportunity to serve.

REFRESHMENTS

Special celebrations, like a Young Authors' Conference, *scream* for cake and punch or any delightful refreshments that go with your theme. After parents go on a tour of the school to see student displays, they can stop by the cafeteria or media center to enjoy refreshments with their young author. This is a good chance for them to mix with the guest author, other visitors, and staff. Your cafeteria manager might be able to help in the area of refreshments.

ASSEMBLY PROGRAM

An assembly program is the pinnacle of the conference and should recognize and celebrate the talents and accomplishments of your young writers. Every writer who has published something should be recognized with a ribbon and certificate. Since time probably will not permit these all to be given in an assembly, consider giving them earlier in individual classes. Kids can wear their ribbons throughout the day to all events.

One option for your program is to have teachers submit well-written selections weeks earlier to the assembly program committee. Out of these, a number are chosen to be read or presented to the student body. I've had students read these on stage, but I prefer having teachers or special guests read the different author's pieces, so they can be heard and hold the audience's attention.

For instance, your master of ceremonies might announce, "Cordelia Jamblosky." (While she makes her way to the stage, he continues.) "Mrs. Porter will be presenting Cordelia's original short story, *Seven Steps To Go*." Cordelia stands near Mrs. Porter while her story is being read and the audience applauds appropriately when the story is

finished. The student is recognized as the *author*, but her work is *presented* by someone who reads in a loud, expression-filled voice. Of course, there are some instances where students will present their own work, especially if they're producing a puppet play, live drama, video-taped performance, or other specialty.

Try to highlight as many different genres as possible, including video-taped computer books, original songs, slide presentations, etc. The assembly program can be presented several times, tailored to the interests and attention span of different age groups. The crucial thing is for students to have no doubt that writing accomplishment is number one at your school!

COMMUNITY AWARENESS

Yes, the Young Authors' Conference requires quite a bit of planning and preparation, but the results are a wonderful experience for young writers and your entire school. A celebration like this is a powerful way to demonstrate to the community the great importance of kids as *authors.*

LAGNIAPPE

A Little Something Extra

Well, here we are at the end of the book. **DYNAMITE WRITING IDEAS!** was designed to help you empower students to become thinkers, writers, and especially authors. The ability to express ourselves in writing is one of the most influential communication tools we can wield. I believe that by teaching writing you are equipping your students for an on-going education and success in important life situations. Why not make it fun?

Some of the things we do in our classrooms will stick with kids for the rest of their lives. I don't remember all of the lessons she taught, but I'll never forget the way I felt when Mrs. Ferguson read my poetry to the class. I had thick glasses and braids, and no one wanted me on their Red Rover team, but I was an *author*, which was big stuff. When Sister Barbara wrote on my paper, "You should consider having your work published," I vowed to do just that. Teachers changed the way I shaped my life.

Have a great year!

MELISSA FORNEY

P.S. I am always interested in your successes and suggestions for new writing strategies. You may contact me by mail:

Melissa Forney
c/o Maupin House Publishing
P.O. Box 90148
Gainesville, FL 32607

My e-mail address is: CRTVENDV@AOL.com

To set up a **DYNAMITE WRITING IDEAS!** workshop at your school or district, or to order copies of this book, contact Julie Graddy at:

jgraddy@maupinhouse.com   1-800-524-0634